30.00

Better Business Speech

Better Business Speech

Techniques, Tricks, and Shortcuts for Public Speaking at Work

Paul Geiger

ROWMAN & LITTLEFIELD

Lanham • Boulder • New York • London

Published by Rowman & Littlefield
A wholly owned subsidiary of The Rowman & Littlefield Publishing Group, Inc.
4501 Forbes Boulevard, Suite 200, Lanham, Maryland 20706
www.rowman.com

Unit A, Whitacre Mews, 26-34 Stannary Street, London SE11 4AB

British Library Cataloguing in Publication Information Available

Library of Congress Cataloging-in-Publication Data
Names: Geiger, Paul, 1959- author.
Title: Better business speech : techniques and shortcuts for public speaking
   at work / Paul Geiger.
Description: Lanham : Rowman & Littlefield, [2017] | Includes bibliographical
   references and index.
Identifiers: LCCN 2017008416| ISBN 9781538102053 (cloth) | ISBN
9781538102060
   (electronic)
Subjects: LCSH: Public speaking. | Business presentations.
Classification: LCC PN4192.B87 G45 2017 | DDC 808.5/1—dc23 LC record
available at https://lccn.loc.gov/2017008416

∞™ The paper used in this publication meets the minimum requirements of
American National Standard for Information Sciences—Permanence of Paper
for Printed Library Materials, ANSI/NISO Z39.48-1992.

Printed in the United States of America

Contents

Acknowledgments

I have always marveled at artistic creativity; in other words, creating something that previously was never there, but yet it was. I am a firm believer that in order to have an understanding of something, we have to already know it on some level. The true messengers bring these things into our awareness. The very definition of awareness is "knowledge of a situation or fact." The following people already know what I am about to say on some level, but I feel compelled to make them truly aware anyway.

I want to thank my parents, Paul and Betsy Geiger, for showing me the strength to endure and the humility that allows for real learning.

It should come as no surprise that it is my children, Jessica, Shaun, and Brian, who inspire me to be the best version of myself—everyday!

I am truly grateful for my dear friend, Ray Andersen, who reminds me that there are so many beautiful ways to look at the world. He is the entrusted guardian of my creative spirit.

Please allow me to praise Jim and Molly Perry for their unending faith, support, and trust. They asked the question, "What do you really want to do?" And this time, I was ready with an answer.

I want to thank the universe for connecting me with Al Pittampalli, who planted the seed for this project when he spoke the prophetic words, "When you decide to write your book, let me know." Until then, I had never even considered adding "author" to my CV.

My wonderful teachers and coaches over the years must also be acknowledged. They have all been traveling on a similar journey to figure out how to communicate the noblest aspects of life and then how to share that ability with as many kindred spirits as possible.

Heartfelt appreciation must go out to the wondrous Tim Phillips, whose acting method taught me how important it is to stay grounded in your body, follow your impulses, and remain truthful and authentic.

I am indebted to all of my clients through the years who brought their challenges and then trusted me to find a practical answer. Their needs forced me to follow my intuition, dig a little deeper, and create a better way.

My colleagues at New York Speech Coaching are without peer. In particular, Justin Stoney, John West, and Alaina Fragoso have been amazingly supportive and understanding of the time and focus that was required to complete this project.

I cannot thank Suzanne Staszak-Silva at Rowman & Littlefield enough for recognizing the need for a book like *Better Business Speech* and being my champion.

Finally, I dedicate this book to my amazing wife, Jan. Her spirit has inspired me and moved me since the day I met her. Yes, my heart is in this book, but ultimately, it is in her hands.

Introduction
The Shortest Distance

Authenticity trumps intelligence! There, I said it, or rather, I wrote it. Trust me, I have said it many times, most often to my speech clients looking for the fastest way to promote themselves in business. Don't get me wrong. Intelligence is a wonderful thing to have. But if you can't communicate your ideas with a sense of confidence and authenticity, no one will believe in them. But how do you become an authentic speaker when you can't seem to get past the discomfort and anxiety of public speaking?

The perception of being an authentic speaker is generated by just two things: owning your breathing and bumper stickers. The first thing seems pretty simple. We all breathe constantly; we ought to be pretty good at it. But most people don't breathe very efficiently, and they certainly don't know how to access the true power of their breath for speech. Breathing and breath support are the keys to the projection and enhancement of your voice. Remarkably, they can be both your physical relaxation and your forward momentum, all at once.

Bumper stickers is the term I use to describe concise messages. A bumper sticker always includes your understanding and perspective, and it is short enough to fit on the back of a car bumper. It isn't an elevator pitch; they're much too long. The discipline of finding and using bumper stickers leads to clarity of thought and the increased confidence many refer to as Executive Presence.

You gain confidence when you gain control of your speech technique. Knowing there are steps you can take begins the process of empowering each individual to become more expressive and more persuasive in a truthful and authentic way. The approach is both physical and mental—breathing and bumper stickers!

There are many books on speech, the voice and public speaking out there—many boring books. Through my years of teaching I have learned to distill the massive amounts of speech and phonetics information into usable concepts with actionable steps and exercises. Even my eyes glaze over when I see someone trying to "cover it all"—and I'm a voice geek! What most people want is a guide that shows them how to use speech coaching in a practical way. My very simple approach is: relaxation leads to comfort, which leads to confidence. Of course, there is a certain amount of trust involved too. You have to trust your impulses, you have to trust your perspective, and you have to trust this approach enough to be willing to change for the better.

1

Speaking Up
(Meetings and Conference Calls)
Meeting Challenges

Meetings and conference calls are an unfortunate obligation of every businessperson's weekly (if not daily) routine. If your desire is to promote yourself and your ideas, you have to not only show up—you have to speak up. The ability to present yourself during meetings and conference calls requires the same attention to technique as improving the sound of your voice, except that the stakes are higher. You might not have an issue with your voice, but confidence in your speech technique is crucial to your success. You need to rely on it to make a strong start and keep people's attention. First impressions and subsequent perceptions have a tendency to last. It can be frustrating to feel as if you haven't lived up to your expectations or your potential.

Meeting Challenge #1 is knowing when to jump in. You are expected to contribute during meetings and conference calls. There is no way around it. Sometimes a segment of a meeting is your responsibility; other times you simply need to look for your opportunities. The reality is that your career depends on it. But there are physical and mental obstacles that can make it difficult to feel comfortable with jumping in and speaking up. You might feel as if the moment of relevance for your comment has already passed, which of course it has. Your comments can often feel as if they are coming out of nowhere, interrupting the current flow of dialogue. The anticipation of that sudden rush of attention when it's your turn can also tend to hold you back.

Meeting Technique A is to never start in neutral. Being physically and mentally ready to contribute is more than half the battle. On the physical side, you can rely on the forward momentum of speaking on breath and the utilization of supportive gestures. On the mental side you need to harness the power of making your spoken ideas bold, concise, and clear.

Breathe deeply in anticipation of jumping in. Allow those deep breaths to connect you to your impulses that will lead to the appropriate gesture. You will also need that breath to project your voice to the room. An unsupported voice can sound strident and whiny and lacks confidence.

Whether you prepare them ahead of time or shape them on the fly, your statements should be bold! Immediately making your point gets people's attention and grounds you in what you're saying. Your listeners then have the opportunity to ask you for additional reasons and elaborations.

Physical and mental forward momentum is especially important during conference calls. Try to stand and even walk around whenever possible. It will have a positive effect on the tone of your voice and will increase your feeling of engagement and energy.

Meeting Technique B is to learn the art of retracing. Retracing means going back to a point that was made earlier. It gives everyone listening a frame of reference regarding what you're about to say. The art of retracing is essentially knowing that you are within your rights to do it. Your tone should be inquisitive, as if you are requesting further elaboration on the topic. Open with phrases such as: "Just to go back to a point we covered earlier . . . " or "I have another thought on the topic of . . . " Make sure the second part of the sentence includes your perspective and is very clear and concise. This approach helps reduce the perception that your comments are coming out of left field and increases your confidence in delivering them.

For added emphasis, direct your initial gesture toward the individual most connected to the topic of your statement. Whether you agree with them or not, you will be engaging them in the dialogue. Supportive gesturing always sends a strong message of your commitment to the words you're saying.

Meeting Challenge #2 is dealing with the feeling of being judged. It is interesting that a performance review is based on the work you do and also on how you present yourself. You project your business persona during meetings and conference calls. The words you say and how you say them have the effect of sending perceptions in a positive or a negative direction. With these stakes in mind, it can be difficult to communicate with confidence. It can feel as if "all eyes are on you" and you desperately need to say the right thing all the time.

Meeting Technique C involves riding the energy of attention. The first step is recognizing that there is something called the energy of attention. When one person directs their attention toward you in conversation, you feel their energy. Adding people to the mix increases that level of attention and energy. It is not all in your head. The energy is real, and everyone has to deal with it. Don't let this initial wave of energy rob you of your confidence. It can often be included in an overall feeling of being judged. The energy of attention is something you cannot overcome or ignore. Treat it like the weather and know that it will be there. This is important because it can determine how strong you start and what others' first impressions will be. Avoid the uncertainty that comes with not knowing about the energy of attention.

Eye contact has quite an impact on first impressions. Remember that if you can't see them, they're not really seeing you. Give everyone a good opportunity to take you in. Smile with the anticipation of what you are going to say. Feel the energy of attention flow toward you. Take a slow breath . . . and begin.

Meeting Technique D focuses on positive and negative perceptions. Positive and negative perceptions have nothing to do with whether someone agrees or disagrees with your point of view. It has to do with perceived levels of confidence and commitment. The clarity and brevity of the ideas you are presenting are important, but not as important as the tone of your voice, your pace, and your body language. A shaky, unsupported voice lacks the necessary vocal confidence. Speaking too quickly sounds as if you're moving on to the next bit of information without adding your perspective. Your gestures need to be definitive, and your facial expressions should be inquisitive, open, and inviting.

It is important to know that trying to figure out your listeners' perceptions while you are speaking is a nearly impossible task. Don't misinterpret everyone staring at you to mean that they are judging you negatively. Don't allow your perception of their perceptions to keep you from boldly making your point. Remember that the middle ground between positive and negative is uncertainty, which is considered a negative perception in the business world.

Meeting Challenge #3 is getting your point across. Your job at meetings and conference calls is to share your perspective and make your point. Anyone voicing disagreement with you is a signal that you have actually succeeded! Remember, there is no counterpoint without a point. There are some aspects of getting your point across that you have control over, and some that you do not. Regardless of the thoughts you are voicing or the words you are speaking, your perspective has to come through loud and clear. Unlike so many other business scenarios, there is no room here for "hedging your bets."

Meeting Technique E requires that you know your bumper stickers. Many individuals know their subject matter in a meeting backward and forward. But they often leave out the most important piece in their preparation. They forget to include their perspective. So, I teach them to use a very important tool called the *bumper sticker*. The bumper sticker is a short phrase of only a few words; short enough that it can fit on a car bumper. It includes your unique understanding or perception of the material being discussed. It requires asking yourself, "Why is this information, or question, important to me? And why it should be important to my listener?" Tapping into this visceral response to the material is the necessary foundation for creating a truly compelling narrative. It isn't hard to revisit this concept during your speech and therefore emphasize your perspective because it includes how you feel about the subject at hand. It also shows a level of passion for what you're doing, a level of commitment that allows your listeners a framework within which to decide for themselves how they feel about the topic and how they relate to it.

Figuring out your bumper stickers is not easy at first, but you will certainly get better at the process through repetition. Start by giving yourself thirty minutes for exploration and discovery. Over time your ability to create strong, concise messages will improve until you will be able to do it at a moment's notice. Now that you know what to look for, sum it up and trim it down!

Meeting Technique F is the proper use of body language. Getting your point across has a lot to do with perceived levels of passion and commitment. This confidence can be projected through the right body language. Your initial gesture and facial expression as you begin to speak sets the tone for everything that follows. Finding a strong initial gesture ties in very nicely with the recent discovery of your own personal bumper stickers. Choose a bumper sticker, take a deep breath, and then say the phrase once, allowing yourself to gesture freely. Repeat this action until you feel more connected to the impulses that will lead you to the most supportive gesture that matches your point. When your intention is clear, your facial expression will also line up with the rest of your body in an appropriate way.

Speech should always be a full body experience. Finding and using good body language is not a parlor trick that makes it only look as if you mean what you're saying; you will feel when your body is in alignment with your spoken thoughts. This technique is one of the simplest ways to overcome the feeling of being held back when you speak.

SMOKE AND MIRRORS (MEETINGS WITH SUPERIORS)

You walk a fine line when you find yourself in a meeting with superiors. You need to be bold in your delivery but also reactionary during the times when you recognize differing communication styles. There is a lot going on and a lot at stake. Your success depends on balancing agendas, responsibilities, and distractions, all while developing your own Executive Presence. Balance truly is the key. You don't want impressions of you to be at either end of the spectrum. You never want to be perceived as too agreeable or too disagreeable, as a "Yes Man" or as a "Loose Cannon."

Your preparation for a meeting is a crucial part of good execution. Taking the time to discover your true perspective and then consistently practicing the delivery of your spoken ideas will improve your execution. This approach leads to increased confidence that people know and trust.

Meeting Challenge #4 is dealing with the distractions. Meetings with superiors are always a big deal. No one takes them lightly. However, there are inherent distractions that can sabotage your success. Most of these distractions come in the form of misconceptions, and many happen prior to the actual meeting. Since you never really know exactly what to expect at any given meeting, there is an overriding feeling of needing to be ready for anything and everything. Piling on the last-minute information in an attempt to project competence is a common preparation mistake. The need to succeed can distract you from your true goal of delivering a clear and concise message. Distractions in execution can range from having a shaky start, to rambling, to being cut short. Getting to the point can be elusive when you feel compelled to prove yourself and inevitably speak too much.

Meeting Technique G is understanding meeting dynamics. The first meeting dynamic you need to be aware of is why you are there. One reason could be because you feel obligated; you were summoned to be there. A second reason might be to take advantage of the face-to-face opportunity and make a good impression. But the real reason you have been called to a meeting with superiors is to act as a filter to distill a large amount of information on your topic of expertise and communicate it in a more concise and digestible form. The clarity of your message is the only way you can show your diligence, understanding, and commitment.

Another general meeting dynamic is that your superiors need you to state your point so that they can then build their counterpoint. Once again the most important thing is to be clear and definitive. You might think that this approach seems a bit presumptuous; after all, he or she is your boss. But remember, they are asking for your opinion—give it to them!

Meeting Technique H is to develop solid bumper stickers. If you have not read about them in earlier in this chapter, *bumper stickers* are the term I use to describe a clear and concise spoken thought. It is a very short sentence or phrase that sums it all up. When delivered with confidence, it boldly states your point of view. There is no room for all of the reasons or information that brought you to your perspective in a short phrase; there may or may not be time for all of that later. This is the distilling process that your superiors are looking for from you. Sift through the information, filter it through your perspective, and deliver the message clearly.

This technique guarantees a very strong start by saying what you need to say right up front. Even if they cut you off, you will have made your point. You will also make strong first impressions as being a straight shooter who knows how to plant the flag in the sand. In most cases you will have an opportunity to elaborate, always returning to your bumper sticker for clarity and connectivity.

Meeting Challenge #5 is communicating with confidence. Meetings with superiors can be intimidating. You know that they are expecting a lot from you, and you are certainly expecting a lot from yourself. Assuming that you have done your due diligence and know the topic of discussion well, your speech technique should support your level of understanding.

You may not even be aware that you are sabotaging your delivery by circling around the topic without landing or by backing off from your perspective. Lack of projection and lack of eye contact can send an unintended message of uncertainty or inability. You may also suffer from speaking too quickly, rambling, or repetitive use of body language that sends unclear intentions. You may be overwhelmed by the fear of saying the wrong thing. The problem is that playing it safe often means making no impression at all. You know you want to commit to the words you're saying, and you don't know what's holding you back.

Meeting Technique I is harnessing effective body language. Facial expressions, gesturing, and eye contact make up over 50 percent of any message you are trying to convey. Body language doesn't just support the message; it often <u>is</u> the message. Most people think the proper use of body language is only an outward projection of confidence. It's true that it is something you show and something people see. It is also an inward feeling of confidence that you can generate in a deliberate way. Remember, you are not "faking it" if your body tells you it's true.

Good body language involves a balance between the right amount of smiling and the right amount of seriousness. Don't be afraid to include some of each in your delivery. In regard to appropriate eye contact, you need to follow the 80/50 rule. Speakers make direct eye contact 50 percent of the time when speaking, and listeners make eye contact 80 percent of the time when listening. In larger groups this actually becomes an easier rule to follow as you move your gaze around the room, only looking at any individual for three to five seconds at a time.

The best way to avoid flailing your arms and forcing your gestures is to breathe deeply at the start of each sentence and allow your natural impulse to create the gesture. Make sure you gesture fully when you practice this technique. Hold each gesture until the impetus for the next gesture comes along.

Meeting Technique J is learning to navigate your perceptions. Perceiving responses as being either negative or positive can either hold you back or move you confidently forward. We are talking about seeing things for what they are and what they are not. For instance, many individuals mistakenly perceive the energy of attention as a sense of being judged, especially by their superiors. They are uncomfortable with the sudden silence and the anticipation of what's coming next. A better approach is to recognize the energy of attention for what it is: an undeniable part of being listened to.

Try to avoid allowing a lack of positive visual response to be a negative perception. It may take a moment or two for your listeners to be comfortable with following along. Their lack of response will mostly come from a sense of empathy than from a sense of judgment. There is also no need to take the temperature of every person in the room while you are speaking. When it is your turn, simply focus on delivery and trust your preparation. See your meetings as opportunities and not simply obligations.

Meeting Challenge #6 is knowing when to reflect and when to be bold. Unlike a presentation, it's hard to predict what might come next in a meeting. You know there will certainly be times when you need to boldly state your perspective, but there will also be times when you need to adapt your communication style to fit the style of your superiors. This can be an enormous challenge to your success. You want your meetings to be an exchange of ideas, but they can often become a battle of personalities. You may find yourself dealing with a boss who is either demanding, sarcastic, blaming, or controlling. It is yet another distraction that can cloud the focus on your agenda and the improvement of your speech technique.

Meeting Technique K is navigating communication styles. Your bosses and managers may use one (or more) of the less-than-desirable communication styles: aggressive, passive-aggressive, submissive, or manipulative. Although they may have found a way to get what they want with this form of communicating, your goal is to remain assertive and clear. Once you become aware of what to look for, you will begin to recognize whether they are responding out of habit or based on the actual presentation of your ideas. Aggressive communicators use intimidation; complaining is a passive-aggressive approach; submissive communicators avoid confrontation; and sulking works for manipulators. When criticism is given, accept it as being constructive. Don't shrink away from it. Maintain your assertive and positive approach.

What you want from a meeting can be different from what your boss or manager wants to achieve. You need to give them the room to set the tone of the meeting while still sending the message that you are ready, willing, and able to share your perspective. This relieves your superiors of the obligation to just tell you your marching orders. Meetings with superiors can be successful when you establish a rapport of confidence and competence.

Meeting Technique L is to never stop developing your own Executive Presence. Executive Presence is a combination of all of the techniques discussed in this chapter: clear thoughts, confident body language, understanding meeting dynamics, and clear perspective on perceptions. The work you do behind the scenes and prior to any meeting prepares you to speak with knowledge, but you need to prepare yourself to deliver like a CEO. Speak your portion of the meeting to become accustomed to the articulation and cadence of your words. Don't just think it through; speak it! Your pace should be controlled and measured. Breathe after each sentence. This will project the sense that you are considering the importance of everything that you're saying. It will also connect you to the impulses that lead to appropriate, supportive gestures and body language. The confidence you need to project is there, you just need to discover it, practice it, and own it.

2

Heavy Lifting
Presentation Challenges

Presentations are the business communication scenarios where you have the most control and the most time to prepare. They also carry the most responsibility and the highest expectations. You not only have the responsibility of setting the tone for the presentation, but you are also expected to be an expert on the subject matter. In an attempt to cover it all, your presentation can become flat and lack engagement. You need to recognize the challenges and avoid the traps already built into every presentation opportunity.

Presentation Challenge #1 is the urge to overstuff. The urge to overstuff a presentation is strong. After all, you have to prove that you're the expert, right? It can feel as if the only way to validate the stating of your point of view is to reveal each step and show all of your work. You know you have a lot of information to get through. You expect that you will lose your listeners' attention if you speak too slowly. So, you hit the ground running and never pause to breathe and give everyone a chance to process what you've said. The truth is that they do want to hear your perspective; they want to hear your opinion. There is no need to prove anything, just the need to deliver with clarity.

Presentation Technique A is to know your three ideas limit. Getting clarity requires that you sum up the reason for your presentation in one short sentence or phrase. My clients are familiar with my term for this phrase—a *bumper sticker*. It is a sentence or phrase short enough to fit on the back of a car bumper. It is the forty-thousand-foot view that sums up your overall message. You don't figure out your bumper sticker as much as you discover it, because it is already there. You probably have lots of great ideas and information about your topic. They all inform your understanding of your bumper sticker. However, one of the most important steps to good preparation is to trim down your presentation to the three most important ideas that brought you to your overall bumper sticker. Three ideas in any one sitting is pretty much everyone's limit. Don't get lost in the light show of additional information. Your presentation is first and foremost about clarity of spoken ideas. A concise message will project a sense of forward momentum that will allow your listeners to recognize that you are in charge. You can always elaborate upon request. Connecting ideas that might be missing for some listeners will certainly come up during the Q&A. That is when you have the opportunity to address them in dialogue form.

Presentation Technique B is the discipline of precise preparation. One of my favorite music teachers was fond of saying, "Practice doesn't make perfect; perfect practice makes perfect." As with most blanket statements, there is a need for some qualifiers here. Perfect practice means preparing the right way. It does not mean that you should expect your presentation to be so perfect that it lacks any sense of spontaneity. Additionally, the goal of preparing perfectly should not keep you from being inspired by new ideas.

Start your preparation by standing up and speaking out loud the reason why you are giving this presentation. The fact that the boss expects you to do it isn't good enough. You need to dig a little deeper. Find the phrase that nails it for you. This is your bumper sticker. Speaking these words out loud will help to connect you to your true perspective on the topic. This is the elusive "being right" part that many people miss. Your point of view is undeniable. Own it.

The next step is to determine the three ideas that best support your perspective. Allow yourself one sentence to describe each idea. Speak each sentence, one at a time, followed by your bumper sticker each time. You need to repeat this process a minimum of ten times until the memory of the connection between the ideas is no longer just in your head but in your body too. Don't make the mistake of spending all of your time just thinking about what you are going to say; really say it!

Presentation Challenge #2 is losing your train of thought. There are several factors that can contribute to losing your way during your presentation. One is suddenly becoming aware that everyone is staring at you and that you are being judged. The second can be the belief that by speaking quicker you will have a better chance of keeping your listeners' attention. Another might be the feeling that you have to fill up all of the "dead air" with nonstop speaking. This rapid, repetitive rhythm is very difficult to maintain. Any break in your pace can send you into recovery mode, which puts you in a state of self-awareness. Another factor can be trying to act in a way that isn't authentic; in other words, acting overly excited or friendly, or trying too hard to be funny. Any of these behaviors can draw your focus away from the primary intention of your presentation and cause you to fall off track.

Presentation Technique C is to let your mind think and your mouth speak. Many public speakers find themselves in a situation in which they're speaking too quickly. They often mistakenly feel as if their minds can't keep up with their mouths. Actually the opposite is true. In the time it takes you to speak one simple thought, your mind is probably thinking about six or seven other thoughts. So, how do you sync these two things up? Let's use the imagery of two conveyor belts: one smaller, slower conveyor belt representing your speech—your articulation—and one larger, faster-moving conveyor belt that presents your thoughts—your mind. Although these two conveyor belts move at different speeds, they intersect each other often. Of course, trusting that they will intersect consistently and effectively requires allowing your mind to think freely while at the same time trusting your speech technique to move at a measured, predictable pace. Ideally we are talking about having balance and trust. If you focus only on speech technique your ideas will come across as practiced, recited, and "canned." Focusing simply on the ideas that flow through your mind will cause you to overstuff your presentation, speak too quickly, and often lose your train of thought.

Step one is becoming aware that this is the way your thinking and your speaking work together. Step two is to practice this technique by actually speaking the words when you prepare. You don't want to be surprised by the sound of your own voice when it comes time to present. Adopt a measured presentational pace. Take the time to notice and explore how much you really can think separate thoughts while you are speaking. You will find that you have more time than you might expect to get yourself back on track.

Presentation Technique D involves the power of the pause. Everyone occasionally needs a moment to regroup and even possibly retrace and revisit their ideas while presenting. Pausing is an extremely effective tool to use for many reasons. When executed in a deliberate and controlled manner, the break in sound can have the effect of grabbing people's attention as they anticipate what will come next. Whether they realize it or not, pausing gives your listeners an opportunity to process what you have just said. Pausing gives you the room to integrate a new thought as it occurs to you. This seems to fly in the face of the common misconception that you should never stop or even slow down your pace for fear of losing your audience.

There are several things you can do to make pausing while you speak look and feel more natural. The first thing is to give yourself permission to do it. Trust me when I tell you that it looks a lot better than it feels. Making it feel better requires that you accompany the pause with a deliberate breath or a sustained gesture. Either of these actions will give you the time you need to collect your thoughts. They also signal to your listeners that you are truly thinking about what you're about to say or that they should pay attention to what you have just said.

Presentation Challenge #3 is working with a deck. How you handle your deck of slides is crucial to the success of your presentation. Problems occur when you rely too heavily on the slides themselves to get your point across. Slides consistently steal focus from you. So, you will find yourself constantly having to reengage with your audience. In truth, your slides are never as interesting as you can be. They are simply the information that reinforces your perspective.

Presentation Technique E is to build anticipation. When you have decided that slides will be a part of your presentation, use them to the fullest. Create anticipation by speaking about either the challenge that the information on the next slide will magically solve or state a rhetorical question that your next slide will clearly answer. Try to avoid overusing the phrase *what we have on our next slide. . . .* This sends the message that your presentation will just be an exercise in looking at projected slides. By building the anticipation you are instructing your audience when to take a quick look at the slides as an overview. They should then be compelled to look back at you for the explanation or clarification of what they're looking at and why it is important. You need to do this to allow your presentation to develop as a narrative. You are the storyteller; you lend the necessary perspective. The slides are just the facts of the story.

Presentation Technique F involves controlling the focus. The first thing you need to consider in regard to focusing your listeners' attention is scale. I don't simply mean the size of the projection screen but also the size of your audience and the space you are presenting in. Make sure your initial gesturing is appropriate for the amount of attention that is being focused on you. Don't shrink away from it. Accept the responsibility of being more important to the presentation than your slides.

Never read the information on the slide word for word. This could be perceived as being disrespectful. We can all read! It defeats the purpose of sharing your personal perspective. Even though you may have put all of the slides together and they clearly reflect your work and perspective, your listeners need to hear the concepts directly from you to allow for the best comprehension. Feel free to step in front of the screen at times as a means of regaining focus and making your delivery more personal.

When working with a team of presenters, make sure your individual roles are clearly defined. Audiences don't mind changing their focus from one presenter to another, but they need to know why they are being asked to do it.

3

Putting Yourself Out There (Networking and Job Interviews)

Networking Challenges

Successful networking and job interviewing is all about connecting. You connect by clearly sharing your perspective. But most people are not completely comfortable with talking about themselves and their unique point of view. There is a fear of sounding boring, or possibly sounding pretentious. You achieve that elusive balance between sharing and bragging by telling the right stories.

Networking Challenge #1 is knowing what to talk about. It can be extremely daunting to determine what the right thing to talk about is at a job interview or networking event. The goal is to come across as professional and friendly in your conversations. Many times these interactions fall flat or don't ever seem to really get off the ground. This can make the attempt feel like an enormous waste of time. How can you possibly determine what will interest one individual but not impress another?

Networking Technique A is to choose the experience over the information. Avoid the temptation to simply regurgitate the facts on your résumé. The who and where of your academic and work experience is there in black and white. Focusing only on the facts can sound redundant at job interviews and like bragging at networking events. You need to add perspective. You need to clearly share what those experiences meant to you. This approach will make you undeniable. No one can tell you it doesn't matter to you.

The importance of your experiences will certainly change in a year or even five years. Therefore, the retelling of the experience will become richer with your deeper understanding. Then again, a new experience may come along to replace the older experience in emotional importance. Do not be surprised by an initial feeling of vulnerability. The best storytellers are invested in their stories. They are willing to reveal their personal perspectives and shine a light on their true personalities.

Networking Technique B is to choose your stories wisely. Telling stories is how you can talk about yourself without making it obvious that you are talking about yourself. Your stories should reflect some aspect of your perspective on the world. Your stories are not simply observations or judgments. Even a story about that day's commute to work can be useful if it reveals how you look at things. Being able to include your point of view in a lighthearted yet thoughtful way is a discipline that can be developed through daily practice. Begin the process by considering these three stories from your life: the Mentor Story, the Leadership Story, and the Overcoming Challenges Story.

The Mentor Story describes that person in your life who saw something in you that inspired them to guide you; they took you under their wing. In reality, you chose them as well. Take the time to explore how much they impacted your life and gave you a direction. Feel free to detail how much you had to learn and how much you did learn. This is a very powerful story because it can highlight your strengths and show your awareness and appreciation of others. Everyone can relate to being influenced by someone, even if it was from afar.

The Leadership Story is not ultimately about what you accomplished but more about the taking on of the responsibility. It is a story about you stepping up. It can be work or school related or focus on your involvement in the community. This story may come from interactions with your immediate or extended family. We have all had these moments in our lives. Take the time to find the one that resonates with you.

The Overcoming Challenges Story is mostly about a personal victory, no matter how small. It doesn't have to be grand or impactful; it just needs to matter to you. The story could describe doing something you always wanted to do or overcoming a fear. Even if your listener doesn't have the same desire or fear, they can relate to the feeling of taking on something that has consistently been in their thoughts.

Networking Challenge #2 is knowing how to insert your stories. You may have no idea how to fit the stories that define you into a conversation or a job interview. Once you know clearly what your stories are, your responsibility is to watch for opportunities to segue into them. Whether you are responding to a question or changing topics, you need to become accustomed to using your stories in a way that seems natural and unforced. This will only happen if you look for your chances and make it happen.

Networking Technique C is using your stories as the answer to any question. The most difficult questions to answer in job interviews are the open-ended ones. Top on the list is, "So, tell me a little bit about yourself." (This isn't actually a question but a very common request.) Because of the nontechnical nature of the request, it is the perfect opportunity to use one of your stories. You only need one sentence to smoothly reach your goal. If you want to lead with the Mentor Story, you might respond, "I was able to truly define my career path while I was working with my mentor." Then tell your story. You could segue into the Leadership Story by saying, "I have been in some situations where I really needed to grab the bull by the horns." You can lead into talking about Overcoming Challenges with the statement, "Some of the things I've wanted to do have required a bit more effort than others."

Once you become comfortable with the right words and phrases, feel free to get creative with your one-sentence lead-in. Look at lists of sample interview questions online and figure out which of your three stories could be a good fit. For some questions, it could be all three.

Remember that no matter how long you take circling around the right way to respond, it will always come down to just one sentence that will lead to the telling of the story. Learn to start with this sentence and be bold! This technique is crucial to standing out at a job interview. For instance, the Mentor Story answers many questions before they can even be asked. It shines a light on some of your best qualities. It shows gratitude and the understanding of the importance of mentoring someone in the future. These are qualities most employers are looking for.

Every interaction at a networking event is basically a "tell me a little bit about yourself" moment. Go in armed with the three stories that define you and look for every opportunity to use them.

Networking Technique D is using your stories from a neutral position. Creating the opportunities in a conversation to insert your three stories can be a difficult technique to master. You will often find yourself in need of this technique at networking events. It requires equal amounts of curiosity and vulnerability. There are times when you have to become the one who asks the opening question or makes the opening statement. Both need to lead to the telling of the stories that define you. It may seem like a long leap from introducing yourself to talking in a more personal way, but it can be done.

The easiest way to generate relatable curiosity is by asking the right rhetorical question. This is a question that you already have an answer for. You could steal this effective approach from the comedian Jerry Seinfeld by using the phrase, "Have you ever noticed . . . ?" This opening rhetorical question works because it assumes a level of understanding by your listener. You are acknowledging that they can relate to the scenario and that they can relate to you.

Vulnerability can be projected by showing a willingness to share your experiences and your perspective. The confidence of knowing what you want to talk about is the key to being able to do this well. Try using a good all-purpose statement like, "This gathering (topic, conversation) reminds me of the time . . . " You will be connecting your current circumstances with an experience from your past, allowing your perspective to shine through. This is a very clear invitation for your listener to relate to the story you are telling.

Networking Challenge #3 is knowing when enough is enough. Long-winded stories are a problem at job interviews and especially at networking events. Until you are able to master your storytelling technique, you will be hard-pressed to keep your listener's attention for an extended amount of time. There may be times when you wonder why a perfectly good story falls flat and doesn't resonate. This often comes accompanied with the awareness that you and your conversation partner are stuck. Ideally, conversations should be very fluid. So, how do you know when you're headed for the wall? Well, you don't and you won't. Therefore, you have to be prepared to adjust your story length on the fly, based on each individual situation.

Networking Technique E is to know the button for each story. The "button" on a story is like the punchline to a joke. It is the ending sentence or phrase that sums up the reason for telling the story and satisfies the initial curiosity created by the bumper sticker you used at the beginning. Buttons don't have to be humorous or witty, but they do have to reveal an aspect of your perspective. The best buttons clearly state the lesson that you learned from the experience. Self-deprecating humor is a wonderful thing to discover in the developing of your button. Always choose the lighthearted ending that will allow your listener to nod along with a sense of understanding. A strong button puts closure on your story and gives an individual the opportunity to change the subject, elaborate on the subject based on personal experience, or politely wrap up the conversation. Here are some general buttons that can work for many stories. Avoid using each one more than once in a conversation: "I didn't realize at the time what a big deal it would be." "I'll never try that again!" "Well, you live and you learn."

Networking Technique F is being able to tell your stories in three different lengths. Most people consider only one way of telling a story. I recommend exploring how to tell your stories in three different lengths. The recommended lengths are: thirty seconds, ninety seconds, and three minutes. Start with the three-minute version. Choose your story, determine your bumper sticker, and develop your button. Begin your story, and keep an eye on the clock. Force yourself to state the button right before the three-minute mark. You will learn to condense the important facts of the story into a streamlined presentation. Do the same for your ninety-second version and your thirty-second version.

Please don't expect to do something well unless you practice it; and by practicing I mean speaking it out loud. Remember, your mind and your mouth consistently move at different speeds. There will be an urge to overstuff, especially if you know there are three versions of your story and you want to give your listener as much as you can at every opportunity. It's understood that you really want to impress every individual you speak with. Impress them with your ability to share the stories that define you without hogging the spotlight. Like the telling of a good joke, timing is everything.

4

Sealing the Deal
Sales Call Challenges

Many businesspeople consider *selling* to be a bad word. They will often say, "Don't try to sell me on the idea!" However, businesspeople are always looking for an opportunity. They intuitively know that if you remain status quo you are actually falling behind. Think of each and every sales call as an opportunity—for them! You are helping very busy business-people not fall behind. Obviously, getting them to give you time in their busy day can be a combination of mood, need, and luck. Make sure you practice describing the opportunity in one simple phrase. This can be challenging, but it is essential for getting them to listen further. Get right to the point over the phone or via e-mail. Avoid the urge to overstuff. Leave enough to the imagination that your potential client will need to ask a follow-up question or two. Your success depends on creating this level of engagement.

Sales Call Challenge #1 is establishing trust. One of the first things clients look for is a sense of being able to trust you. This can be difficult to establish when they are so wary of salespeople. They certainly don't want to seem too eager, too soon. They know that you are watching them, looking for signs that you can move forward. You know they are watching you closely too. The awareness of the scenario can cause you to act in a less-than-confident manner, which can be misinterpreted as a lack of commitment to the ideas you are sharing. Trying to be "bigger, better, faster, more" is not the approach that works in establishing trust. Your personal commitment to the things you are saying has to come through loud and clear. You can't move forward without it.

Sales Call Technique A involves finding the common ground. Doing your due diligence in preparation for a sales call will allow your curiosity regarding this individual or company to flourish. Even if your research has been extremely thorough, allow your client to tell you something you don't already know. Give them the opportunity to share their perspective. Don't be afraid to lead with your curiosity; it may take the conversation in an unexpected direction. You show you are genuinely interested by pausing and asking questions of inclusion early and often. Your questions should require an experiential answer that allows the client to relate their story to you and the opportunity you are presenting.

You can certainly agonize over the need to close the deal in preparation, but once you are in the sales call, you have a different goal to focus on—connecting with your client. Always think in terms of building a relationship with this person. Personalize the presentation by including your experiential information. Ask if your client can relate to your perspective on the experience.

Sales Call Technique B is to raise your authenticity quotient. Authenticity does not refer to proving that you are qualified as an expert. It is the perception that you are ready, willing, and able to share your perspective. There are several things you can do to raise the level of your perceived authenticity. Speak slowly and clearly. Even though you may think that your clients are looking at you with a "time is money" expression on their faces, no one really likes to listen to a "fast talking" salesperson. Integrate deliberate breathing into all of your communications. This will send a message that you are truly considering your words and their importance.

Body language is another key to slowing you down. Gesturing fully will not only give the perception that you are connected to what you're saying but it will also allow you to punctuate choice words and slow down your pace.

Eye contact is important in the right amounts. Always follow the 80/50 rule of making direct eye contact: 80 percent when listening and only 50 percent when speaking. You have to give your listeners enough unguarded moments when you are not looking at them to allow them to look in on your thought process and relate to the story you're telling. Unguarded moments exude confidence and authenticity.

Facial expressions should be warm and accessible. Avoid smiling too much in an effort to be overly friendly and accommodating. No one smiles all the time, and everything isn't always funny. Spending hard-earned money is serious business. Be aware of finding the balance that lets multiple levels of your passion, commitment, and sense of humor to come through.

Sales Call Challenge #2 is staying clear and confident. There is so much to keep track of during a sales call. You have to establish trust, integrate new questions, watch for subtle signals, and deliver your message with the right inflection and nuance. You want to come across as energized and enthusiastic without seeming as if you want to "steamroll" anyone. Your client's questions, and subsequent answers, can have the effect of taking the conversation off on a tangent. How you recover and push forward has an enormous impact on your ability to achieve your goals.

Sales Call Technique C involves knowing the structure of your agenda. Sales calls are different from the other business communication scenarios in that it doesn't serve you to reveal your bumper sticker right up front. Your bumper sticker is that single phrase that sums up why this opportunity is such a good idea. Every bumper sticker should be supported by no more than three reasons. Choose the reason that you believe your client will be able to relate to the best. Slowly integrate the other two reasons during the sales call, and allow the revealing of the bumper sticker to happen right before you ask for their commitment. This level of preparation and execution will be your anchor in a sea of variables. You can never predict what a client's questions or responses will be. Always look for the opportunity to segue into some part of your agenda. This approach will keep the conversation on track and keep you from overstuffing with too much information.

Sales Call Technique D requires recognizing the behavior of engagement. You can gain confidence by knowing that your client's behavior has to go through a transformation during the sales call. They may appear to be skeptical at first. Recognize this as part of the process. Everyone needs time to understand a new perspective and determine how they relate to it. Don't allow your confidence to erode because you are misreading your client's body language. Short answers to your questions of inclusion do not always mean they are becoming disengaged. There is a very good chance they are processing what you are presenting to them. Allow the process to unfold. When your client becomes less talkative, it usually means they are going along with what you're saying.

. *Sales Call Challenge #3 is delivering persuasion.* You can sometimes leave a sales call feeling as if it wasn't very effective. Your spoken ideas may have been crystal clear. Your client's body language and responses may have indicated that they were very engaged. All of the aspects of delivering your presentation were on point, but you did not achieve the results you were looking for. Ultimately, your goal is to deliver persuasion. It can seem as if the timing involved in doing this effectively and consistently can be very elusive.

Sales Call Technique E is to be aware of the different steps that lead to persuasion. Persuasion requires that two participants in a conversation reach the same mindset at the same time. The steps that lead to persuasion are a little different for you than they are for your client. Recognizing and aligning these different sets of steps can be where true connectivity occurs.

Your steps to persuasion are: energy, clarity, comfort, confidence, momentum, and persuasion. Energy is required to move the conversation in an initial direction. Clarity comes from customized preparation. Comfort is both a feeling and a projected perception of owning your spoken thoughts. Confidence is establishing that you are the one driving the bus. Momentum is the building of one idea onto the next. Finally, persuasion is the clear sharing of your perspective.

Your clients' steps in a sales call vary slightly. They are: consideration, focus, confidence, momentum, and persuasion. Consideration is more than just taking a look. It involves building trust in you and your message. Focus means seeing the opportunity through the framework you are providing. Confidence is their knowing that you believe in what you're saying. Momentum is the repeated unfolding of why the opportunity makes sense. Persuasion is their belief in your perspective.

You need to give your clients time to think for themselves and go through the necessary steps. Your energy, clarity, and comfort should warrant their consideration. Your confidence will help them focus. As you build momentum, their confidence will rise. The momentum of the unfolding will allow your client to understand and believe in your perspective. These steps bring you and your client to not just the moment of believing but a moment of doing!

Sales Call Technique F is to ask for what you want at the right time. In order to succeed at sales, you have to be able to ask for what you want. In preparation for the sales call, practice how you will complete the sentence, "I want you to (blank)." Be wary of inserting words that sabotage the momentum you have taken the time to develop. "I want you to consider . . . ," "I want you to think about . . . ," or "I want you to look at . . ." should never be a part of your "ask." The time for considering or thinking about the opportunity was earlier in the sales call. Now is the time for action and commitment.

Of course the timing of your ask is as important as how you phrase it. Once you have followed through on the steps of persuasion, reveal the bumper sticker that sums up how you view this opportunity. Then clearly and authentically state what you want your client to do. Sales calls are conversations that require a call to action. In the end, your statement must be bold. Know why you would commit and share that understanding with your client. This will give you permission to ask genuine questions if objections arise.

5

Realizing the Problem
Personal Complaints

It can be very difficult to speak confidently in business if you are not comfortable with your voice. You certainly know what the discomfort feels like, but you probably don't know why it is happening. Speech patterns can be hard to break, but it is encouraging to know that there are things you can do to increase your comfort and clarity.

I speak too quickly!

What it feels like. Fast talking can be hard for an individual to recognize due to many of the misconceptions there are about speech. Feeling the need to fill up the empty space between words and sentences with sound can be part of the problem. You may also feel like your brain is just trying to keep up with your mouth. You may anticipate that your listeners won't understand your message, so you need to repeat it several times at a very fast pace. Many individuals mistakenly believe that the faster you talk, the smarter you sound. There are some who believe that the faster you talk, the more exciting you will sound. At some point you realize that none of these common justifications for speaking quickly leads to desired results.

Becoming aware that you are speaking too quickly can feel as if you're on a runaway train with no means of slowing down. You can't wait for your presentation or conversation to be over, which makes things even worse. You may start to feel nervous. This will cause your speed to continue to increase. Once you have established a fast rate of speech, slowing down is no longer an option. You know that that would just bore your listeners to death.

Speaking quickly will definitely have an effect on the way your listeners feel, influencing their perceptions. There are several negative perceptions that can be associated with talking too fast. It can make you look as if you're trying to prove that you're more intelligent than your listeners. By not giving anyone else any room to jump in, you may come across as wanting to hog the spotlight. Speaking too quickly can actually make you seem insecure and nervous. This perceived inability to put on the brakes can make you seem as if you're out of control.

Why it happens. There are many reasons why people speak too quickly. First of all, many people don't like the sensation of speaking and often speak too quickly in situations in which they just want the scenario to end because of discomfort. The sense of freedom and confidence that comes with good vocal balance is missing. Speaking quickly will not hide this fact. Sufficient breath is required to create sound. An individual who knows how to use that breath effectively and efficiently is considered to have vocal balance.

There is a part of your brain that monitors whether you have enough air in your lungs to complete your spoken thoughts. It encourages you to hurry up because you are consistently running low on vocal fuel, which is air. Since most people simply do not breathe deeply or often enough, there is a constant physical pull to speak quickly.

Many people maintain accelerated pace when speaking because they're afraid of losing their listener's attention. This insecure thought process can convince you that if you keep revving up the pace of what you're saying, your listeners will continue to be interested in who you are.

Lack of trust that your mind and your mouth can work together at different speeds can also cause you to speak too quickly. You need to have confidence in your speech technique. I don't mean having confidence in your technique for giving speeches but your everyday vocal technique. Your mind and your speech definitely work at different speeds. You can think many thoughts in the time it takes you to speak just one idea. You don't want your brain and your mouth to slow down or speed up for each other at all!

So you can see that if all of these physical conditions exist, it can be pretty hard to slow down. Many individuals are not connected to their breathing and their breath support, therefore they are always "low in the tank." Most people never consult with a speech coach and therefore don't have any idea how to slow down without making their delivery sound choppy and out of character. When I say speaking slowly or slowing down our speech, what I mean is taking the time to pause in between sentences and phrases, taking the time to breathe more deliberately, and therefore giving the perception of being more thoughtful. Your spoken words need to have more gravitas, or weight. Being able to do this smoothly is essential to speaking at the proper pace.

What to do. The first step toward slowing down the pace of your speech technique is to integrate more deliberate breathing into your everyday communications. The next time someone asks you a simple question, take a very deliberate breath, hold that breath for a moment, and then answer. You will be surprised by what breathing does—and doesn't do. Deliberate breathing does not reveal nervousness. Quite the opposite is true! You will definitely give the impression that you are either truly considering your words, that what you're about to say is important to you, or that you are a thoughtful and poised individual. There is no negative perception associated with breathing deliberately. This is important to understand because it gives you permission to breathe deeply and integrate that breathing into your communication style. Good breathing and proper breath support are the simplistic answers to most speech problems. It is more than OK to own it and use it!

Now that I've convinced you to breathe deeply, let's look at where you need to put all of that breath. Most people can figure out that you need more air when you want to get louder, but good breath support is also needed to create and maintain vowel space. Your mouth and your nasal cavities are where your voice lives. There are distinct spaces where each vowel sound is meant to resonate. There are twelve different vowel positions in American English. Some are long: *ee*, *ay*, *aa*, *ah*, long *oo*, *oh*, and *au*; and some are short, or clipped: *ih*, *eh*, *er*, *uh*, and short *oo*. The twelve different vowel positions can also be divided into high vowels: *ee*, *ih*, *ay*, *eh*, *er*, *uh*, long *oo*, and short *oo*; and low vowels: *aa* (as in *bat*), *ah* (as in *Bob*), *au* (as in *ball*), and *oh* (as in *boat*). It is this last group of lower, elongated vowels that we want to focus on. They are the vowels that require more space in our mouths. When speaking the vowels—*aa*, *ah*, *au*, and *oh*—you need to relax your jaw, and open up and recognize that they have a bigger breath support obligation than the other vowels. This combination of awareness and execution is what we call creating and maintaining good vowel space. It will certainly have the positive effects of slowing your pace, giving your voice more resonance, increasing your projection, and allowing the musculature around your larynx and vocal cords to relax. (Vocal cords are also referred to as vocal folds.) By becoming more vowel centric in your speech approach, you will actually be able to use the language itself as a means of slowing down. Well-supported vowels are essential to developing good vocal balance.

You can also improve your vocal balance by learning how to "put on the brakes." The stopping and starting of speech is controlled using your diaphragm muscle. Your diaphragm is located right below your lungs. Its job is to push up on your lungs when speaking. This motion then pushes the air up through your esophagus. Yes, this is also how we breathe 24/7! The engaging of your vocal cords is what makes sound. No air means no sound. Your diaphragm becomes the brakes you need to slow yourself down. Try saying this sentence, pausing for a full second at both ellipses: "It doesn't have to be . . . this . . . way."

You should feel a little tug or squeezing of your diaphragm muscle with each pause. Now you know where your brakes are located and how to use them. Additionally, you will be harnessing the power of the pause. It is a wonderful example of the physiology of speech adding emphasis to a message. Only you need to know that what you're really doing is just trying to slow down.

I speak too softly!

What it feels like. Speaking too softly and not being able to project your voice is a very common vocal complaint. Always being asked to repeat or always being asked to speak up can really erode your confidence. It can actually lead to a decrease in the desire to speak at all! When you do muster the courage and energy to raise your voice it can sound as if you're shouting at your listeners. You have a feeling of diminished presence and a lack of confidence in your ability to share your thoughts and perspectives. You worry that you will be perceived as weak, noncommittal, or even unsure. At times your voice can sound breathy or puffy. The thin sound of your voice limits your freedom to express yourself, and you worry that the discomfort you feel is plainly visible and being misinterpreted as disagreement with another's point of view. You wonder why many of your conversations have a tendency to be short and lack engagement.

Loud environments are an enormous challenge. You struggle with being understood or even heard at all. This is often accompanied with the tense feeling of straining your voice, which can lead to vocal fatigue.

Why it happens. As much as we think being a soft talker is all in our heads, this perceived "shyness" is really due to an imbalance in our bodies. The fuel for your voice is your breath. Shallow breathing leads to a shallow voice. An unsupported voice can feel choked due to the muscles around your larynx and vocal cords squeezing in an attempt to help out. Everyone has made some sort of physical adjustment due to a lack of breath support that now feels like normal speech behavior. This repeated speech behavior can have the effect of squeezing the life out of your voice over time.

To achieve a bigger sound you need a bigger acoustic environment. For speech, that acoustic environment is your mouth. Most people don't open their mouths as much as they should or could. Limited breath support and constricted acoustic space are the primary causes of poor vocal balance. Your speech is not flowing easily "on breath."

Not breathing deeply and not opening your mouth enough are only part of the problem. Treating all of your vowel sounds the same will also lead to vocal imbalance. Most don't realize the breath support obligation for the lower, elongated vowel sounds. In American English, a lot more breath energy is required to fill the vowel space of *aa*, *ah*, *au*, and *oh* than is required to speak the vowels *ih*, *eh*, and *uh*.

The last part of the puzzle has to do with leaking air. There are several reasons for air leakage. The most common one is pushing too much air into voiceless consonant sounds. The difference between voiceless and voiced consonant sounds is that voiced consonant sounds are made by engaging the vocal cords while voiceless sounds do not. Therefore, the voiced consonant sounds—*B*, *D*, *V*, *G*, *Z*, *ZH*, *DJ*, and voiced *TH*—have more natural resonance and are louder than the lighter voiceless sounds *p*, *t*, *f*, *k*, *s*, *sh*, *ch*, and voiceless *th*. Trying to make the voiceless sounds as loud as the voiced sounds leads to pushing too much air, overarticulation, and leakage. Additionally, leaking on voiceless consonants will lead to a breathy or puffy sound due to poor vocal cord closure.

What to do. You need to get into better vocal shape. For those of you who can't even find the time to go to the gym, I have good news. This workout uses the sounds you already speak on a daily basis. Vocal balance is achieved through awareness and correct practice.

First, you need to integrate deeper and more deliberate breathing into your everyday communications. I realize that breathing deeply may seem awkward when you're not used to doing it. Trust me. The more you do it, the better it will feel. You cannot expect to suddenly achieve good vocal balance only when you are addressing a large audience or when you need to project your voice in a loud environment. Therefore, breathing deeply has to become an everyday approach to speech. Try breathing deeply before you speak a sentence or answer a question and notice the reaction from your listeners. They will listen more intently to what you're saying because you will be giving off the perception that you are truly considering what you are about to say. The fact that it seems so important and heartfelt to you will lend a sense of importance to them listening to and considering your point of view. Your motivation is to improve your vocal balance. The perceived thoughtfulness is a bonus!

Second, make sure you don't let any of that deep breathing slip away and leak out. After taking a deep breath, hold it for just a moment and then deliberately use it to speak. You can take further control of your diaphragm muscle by consciously starting and stopping your speech. Become aware of how often you already do this in your everyday communications. *Continuity* is the term we use to describe the smooth transition from one articulated sound to the next. One of the most used "continuity tricks" is the *glottal T*. A wonderful example of a glottal T can be found in the word *watch*. Recognize that the T is not articulated as a traditional voiceless T but as a glottal T. Because of similar positioning of the tip of the tongue for many consonant articulations, we often use a glottal T in place of a normal T articulation in the middle and at the end of many words. You execute a glottal T by holding the tip of your tongue on your hard palate and synchronize stopping the airflow using your diaphragm muscle. Now say the short sentence, "It's just not right." Recognize that each word has a T in it, and each of those Ts is articulated as a glottal T. You will feel a tug on your diaphragm and hear a slight gap in sound that indicates where the normal T articulation would be. Every time you do this you are engaging your diaphragm and training yourself to use breath regulation.

Another step toward limiting leakage is to focus on all of the voiced Z sounds disguised as the letter *S*. Whenever a plural S follows a voiced consonant it should be articulated as a voiced Z. Try speaking these words, noticing the plural S is actually a *Z*: *abs, hands, lives, bags, changes, judges,* and *clothes.* Some other very common words that use a voiced Z disguised as S are *is, as, was, has, his,* and the contraction *there's.* Many words spelled with an S actually use the voiced Z. Many go unnoticed even by the most articulate speakers. Becoming "voiced Z conscious" will help you align your articulation and reduce the leakage of air on your voiceless consonant sounds.

Next, you need to create and maintain good vowel space, especially when speaking the lower, elongated vowels *aa, ah, au,* and *oh* and the combination vowel sounds long *i,* as in *my*; *ou* as in *now*; and *oy* as in *boy.* These last three big vowels are examples of a diphthong, which is a blending of two vowel sounds. All of these large vowel sounds require a relaxed jaw and an open mouth.

Finally, you need to recognize the sensation of flowing on breath. By harnessing your vocal power you will notice an increase in the forward momentum and the volume of your relaxed speech.

I hate the sound of my voice!

What it feels like. Changing the sound of your voice requires improving the overall tone of your voice. The most common voice complaint regarding tone is that a voice is too nasal sounding. There are actually two types of nasal voices. A hyper-nasal voice is pushed up in the nose and has too much nasal resonance. It can feel and sound "honky" or brash and unpleasant. A hypo-nasal voice has too little nasal resonance. It can feel and sound "dopey" or like you have congestion from a cold.

Many voice complaints have to do with the feeling that a voice is too high or too low. These feelings are connected to the response of others to the sound of your voice. Men often complain about their voices being too high. They want to avoid being mistaken for a woman over the phone. Many women say they wish their voices were not so low. They have a similar problem in that they are often mistaken for being a man over the phone. Having a high, childlike voice is also a common female vocal complaint. These unintended perceptions can lead to feelings ranging from discomfort to embarrassment.

You may have become aware that you speak in a monotone. This describes a speech pattern in which all of the words have a similar pitch and all of the sentences have the same rhythm.

Why it happens. The tone of an individual's voice is affected by the efficient or inefficient use of their vocal apparatus. Sound is created by moving air out of your lungs using your diaphragm muscle and allowing it to flow past our vocal cords. This causes the vocal cords to vibrate, making sound. This sound is then manipulated by moving your tongue, lips, and jaw and using your teeth, your hard palate, and your soft palate to create articulated speech. Sufficient breath support is needed not only for louder speech but also to develop a fuller and more resonant sound. Individuals with insufficient breathing often compensate by using other muscles surrounding the larynx and vocal cords. This can lead to a "squeezing" of the voice, which causes a higher-pitched sound.

The voice that is too low can also be the result of inefficient breath support. It often has to do with a lack of confidence in exploring the use of the higher pitch and tones of a voice. Breath support is essential to taking the voice higher in an unstrained manner.

Everyone's voice sounds slightly different because vocal cords are different. The size and thickness of an individual's vocal cords has a lot to do with their default, relaxed pitch. Finding increased resonance for your voice is the key to increasing your comfort and confidence. An imbalance in voice resonance can occur when the default position of the back of the tongue is too high or too low. Ineffective speech behavior develops over time and is usually connected to poor breathing and breath support.

A monotone voice is also the result of lacking the breath support needed to confidently explore pitch and execute varied rhythms. Intonation is the combination of pitch and rhythm. Lackluster intonation is the reason for monotone speech.

What to do. If developing a fuller voice is your primary goal, start by making sure that your vocal cords are relaxed and vibrating freely. Take a deep belly breath using your diaphragm. Hold the breath momentarily. Then open your relaxed jaw slowly as you would when being examined by the doctor or the dentist and say "ah." Sustain a comfortable volume for seven to eight seconds. Repeat this exercise several times until the sound becomes flat and no longer wavers. If you can't get the sound to flatten out then try placing the tip of your tongue in front of your bottom teeth and behind your lower lip and repeat the exercise. This will pull your tongue away from the back of your throat slightly, opening up more re-laxed space and allowing your vocal cords to vibrate freely. This is called *clear phonation.*

You can begin to explore pitch by using a similar approach. This time monitor yourself in the mirror. Take a deep breath; hold the breath. Then open your relaxed jaw and make the sound "ah" at a low, relaxed pitch. Slowly raise the pitch, making sure that your jaw does not close as the pitch moves higher. Then let your voice lower again to your starting pitch. Repeat this several times until you can execute the varying pitches smoothly.

Next you need to focus on the lower, elongated vowels: *aa, ah, au,* and *oh,* in your everyday speech. These vowel sounds require a lot of air. They also require that you relax your jaw and give them sufficient vowel space. These are the vowels we use for increasing projection, resonance, and relaxation. Say the phrase, "That's not what I need to hear." Notice how large the vowels of *that's* and *not* and *I* are compared to the other vowel sounds in the sentence. These are the words in the phrase that need the most breath support.

When you know the lower, elongated vowels are coming, it's pretty easy to prepare for them, but you can never be exactly sure what par-ticular words you're going to use next in the course of a conversation or impromptu speech. So, it's important to get in the habit of taking a deep breath whenever you speak. You will then be ready for any large vowels that come along. Now that you know what the breath support obligation is you can see that you will need to breathe more often and much deeper.

Learning to speak "on breath" with better breath support is also the key to improving your vocal balance. It will give you access to a much larger percentage of your natural voice by freeing you of constricted phona-tion due to improper speech behavior. By increasing your resonance and relaxation, you will be increasing your comfort in speaking, along with your confidence.

Being able to count on your breath support is essential to changing a monotone speech pattern. Connect to your body and your breath by using gestures when you speak. Let's use the sentence, "How could you possibly believe that?" Slowly raise both hands with palms up when speaking the first three words, "How could you . . . " Drop both hands to waist height on the word *possibly* and finish the sentence. Repeat the same sentence speaking at a higher pitch on the word *possibly*. You will become aware that feeling the strength of your body underneath you will make it easier to take that raised pitch higher. Repeat the sentence, changing the emphasized word. Synchronize your gesture and raised pitch on the words *how*, *you*, and *that*. Experiment with short sentences and phrases that you use on a regular basis. In a similar manner, you can explore varying the rhythm of your speech. Consistent practice and experimentation will increase your comfort and confidence and bring new life to your sound.

I sound like I don't know what I'm talking about!

What it feels like. Sounding unsure or uncertain comes from the growing awareness that people are not taking you seriously. The lack of flow in a presentation, or even a conversation, further enforces this negative perception. Constant starting and stopping and searching for the right words and the use of filler words, and sounds, such as *like*, *uh*, *um*, *okay*, and *you know*, add to the downward spiral. There is a perceived need to speak more quickly, which makes the use of filler words more frequent. The pauses in your speech seem agonizingly long, and it feels as if there is no end in sight. Like running down a steep hill, you have to keep going and going. It feels like your mind can't keep up with your mouth. Along with that feeling, nothing that you're saying seems to end definitively. In an attempt to connect your spoken ideas, you end each sentence on a rising pitch as if you are indicating to your listener that there is more to come. The problem is that everything you say starts to sound like a question, such as, "I could tell you more? Maybe?" Increasing volume, pace, and the amount of information have no positive effect. Nothing that you say seems to come out the right way. You feel as if you desperately need to connect with your listeners but you don't know how.

Why it happens. Uncertainty in your speech technique happens for several reasons. They all have to do with breath control, perceptions, and preparation. Most individuals are not properly connected to their breathing and have insufficient diaphragm control. Good breath support allows your speech to flow. It is the attempt to make your speech flow without breath support that leads to the use of filler words. There is no sound without air passing our vocal cords and moving out of our bodies. Filler words are sounds that require the same exhalation of breath. You are in charge of when the air moves in and out of your body with your diaphragm muscle. It is both your forward momentum and your "vocal brakes."

The habit of constantly ending your sentences on a raised pitch is referred to as "up speak." Not having enough breath to adequately support large vowel sounds is one cause of up speak. Ending high in pitch when you're running out of breath is a lot easier than ending low. The other cause of up speak is the mistaken belief that you need to maintain the continuity of a thought or storyline in this way. A listener's perceptions of a person using up speak can range from uncertainty to lack of intelligence. It is often associated with someone who speaks without actually thinking things through.

A lack of proper preparation is often at the root of many rambling presentations and conversations. Good preparation requires a clear perspective. Information without a perspective has no point. In an attempt to distance themselves from possibly saying the wrong thing, many individuals will leave their point of view out of their preparation. You may know your material backward and forward, but it must be filtered through your perspective to become a truly compelling narrative.

Trying to fit in too much information can have an adverse effect on your intonation. The combination of the rhythm and the pitch is considered the intonation of your speech. Speaking too quickly leaves very little room to vary pitch and no room to change rhythm. Over time, this can lead to a very narrow band of expression that most people recognize as a monotone voice. Varying your intonation makes what you're saying sound more interesting; it also makes you sound more interested in speaking it. It can be really hard to pay attention to someone who speaks in a monotone.

What to do. The first step toward sounding like you know what you're talking about is to integrate deliberate breathing into your everyday communication style. Try reading out loud from the newspaper, taking a deep breath at the start of each sentence. Then try placing breath marks somewhere in the middle of each sentence, and read each sentence breathing in two places. This will feel awkward at first and the gaps may seem unending, but keep at it! Next, tell a personal story about any life experience—vacation, daily commute, lunch with a friend—and use the same breathing integration technique. Inhalations will soon begin to replace the exhalations needed to produce filler words and sounds. You may not be able to notice a reduction in your use of filler words and a slowing of your pace, but an empathetic listener will.

The elimination of up speak requires the same integration of deliberate breathing. You also need to practice ending on a down pitch in a definitive way. Place a large gap before the last three words of any sentence. Place emphasis on these words as if you are a lawyer speaking confidently in a courtroom. Recognize that you will need to stop and start your airflow in between each word by using your diaphragm muscle.

The next thing to do is consider body language as a continuity device. Some studies say that 50 percent of your message is conveyed through body language, which is the combination of appropriate gesturing and facial expressions. Trust your instincts and your impulses; they will lead you to gestures and expressions that will support what you're saying. Your listeners will hold a thought as long as you confidently hold your gesture. This will give you the time needed to breathe deeply and lock in your next spoken idea.

Take the time in preparation to explore your intonation. Once again you will need good breath support to have the confidence to vary your rhythms and allow your pitch to rise and fall. Don't wait until you are giving your next presentation or you find yourself in an important conversation. If you don't try it out ahead of time, you certainly won't feel good about stepping outside of your comfort zone. Use a simple sentence like, "I have a lot on my plate right now." Place the emphasis on a different word each time you speak the sentence. Listen for how the pitch of each word in the sentence changes slightly depending on proximity to the emphasized word. These are the colors that add nuanced meaning to everything we say. Use similar sentences to pause between different words to change rhythm.

Better preparation in general can be achieved by understanding that a presentation is an invitation to share your perspective about the content. This concept will help to eliminate some of the self-doubt and the questioning of whether you are saying the right thing. You don't necessarily need to know everything there is to know about your subject matter. It is more important to have a clear understanding of what is important to you. Retrace the path of your discovery of the importance of the topic. Choose the three best reasons that support your perspective. Then distill all three reasons into one phrase short enough to fit on a car bumper sticker. This is the message that you will need to return to and reinforce during your presentation or conversation.

People don't understand what I'm saying!

What it feels like. We all have moments when we feel like people are not understanding what we're saying. Consistently feeling that you have to repeat yourself or that you have to explain further can really interrupt the flow of your speech and cause you to lose confidence.

You get the feeling that people are staring as if they're not following you, only to find out later that your listeners received a different message than the one you intended or that they disregarded altogether the importance of what you said. You notice that there is seldom any follow-up engagement after you speak. You sense a lack of connection, even though you know your content very well. This is unexpected feedback with undesirable results. You feel as if you have to do more, that you have to try harder. The truth is you need to do less—with more precision.

Why it happens. The most common reasons for a disconnect with listeners are: overexplaining, unnecessary facial expressions, and poor eye contact. These considerations can really sabotage your speech technique. They can either distract the listener or send an entirely incorrect message. Instead of paying attention to what you're saying, they are noticing how you say it.

Overexplaining can occur when you either lack a concise point to your message or you get lost in the light show of your own information. Overexplaining can take the form of talking too much or excessive repeating. Listeners can only process a maximum of three ideas at a time. Trying to communicate more than three ideas is considered overstuffing and should always be avoided.

Unnecessary facial expressions most often occur due to overarticulation and lack of supportive gesturing. One of the most common unnecessary facial expressions, called spread, occurs when the corners of the mouth widen too far when articulating certain consonant sounds and making certain vowel sounds. Spread can lead to excessive smiling and, in extreme cases, an unwanted baring of the teeth. Excessive smiling can send the message that you are being disingenuous. Baring of the teeth when articulating can send an unwanted message of anger or aggression.

Overactive eyebrows are another unnecessary facial expression. This condition is usually the result of a disconnect from impulses and gesturing. The discomfort in feeling disconnected leads to an attempt to nuance your speech with excessive eyebrow movements. This can send the unwanted message that you are constantly looking for approval or that you are fearful.

Special consideration needs to be given to good eye contact. There is a fine line between too much and too little. The 80/50 rule is a good one to follow. When listening to an individual in a conversation you will probably make direct eye contact 80 percent of the time. When speaking to that same individual, the percentage of eye contact is only about 50 percent. As listeners we want to give the speaker the appropriate respect of attention, but as speakers we need to give our listener an unguarded moment to observe our thought process. Every conversation, meeting, or speech involves the telling of a story. Looking away in thought or as you gather the right words or recall an experience is crucial to connecting as a good storyteller.

What to do. The first thing you need to do is become accustomed to condensing your message into a *bumper sticker*. That's right—a bumper sticker. Your entire speech, presentation, or conversation needs to be summed up in just a few words that can fit on the back of a car bumper. It is the reason you are speaking. It includes your perspective and why what you're about to say is important to you. Everything else will expand from this concise message. The foundation of what you're saying depends on it. Your bumper sticker is the central idea that you will keep returning to. This does not mean you can take a shortcut from doing your due diligence regarding the topic. First, you have to do the work and research the topic sufficiently; then you can explore what you have learned and what it means to you. This will bring you to your bumper sticker. The next step is to determine the three ideas that support your message. You now have the basic outline of your speech or presentation. This is the beginning of doing less with more precision!

Removing the pattern of unnecessary facial expressions is the next step. To monitor for spread, think of keeping your articulation vertical, instead of allowing it to move horizontally. This approach will help to reduce excessive smiling when you're speaking. The vowel sounds to watch out for are *ee*, *ay*, *aa*, and long *i*, which is a combination of *ah* and *ee*. The consonants that are most often overarticulated are voiceless T, nasal N, voiceless S, and voiced Z. Occasionally watch yourself in the mirror to become aware of any unnecessary facial movements. Do not practice exclusively in front of a mirror. This will give you a false sense of visual security that will be not available when you are actually in a particular communication scenario.

Overactive eyebrows are usually a sign of a disconnect from the idea that speech is a full body expression. Understanding how important gesturing is to speech technique is crucial. There are studies that say that over 50 percent of a spoken message is conveyed through body language. So you better get connected to your body fast. The easiest way to do this is through breathing. Take a deep breath, hold it for a moment, and then gesture with both hands as you allow the words to flow out of you. Hold the gesture while you take another deep breath, and gesture once again as you speak. Remember to never let go of a gesture until the impulse for the next gesture comes along. Full expression with gesturing has a tendency to relax your articulators and reduce tension in the face. You really do need to do less, this time with more relaxation.

Better eye contact requires that you improve your ability to look away. You need to become more comfortable and confident with giving your listener that unguarded moment. Pick a spot just slightly to the left or right of the individual you are speaking to. Remember to avoid looking up too high or down too low. Looking too high or too low may cause them to believe you are suddenly looking at something in the room, and this will distract them. The looking away is usually done while breathing deeply, therefore completing the idea that you are simply into your thoughts.

This approach to improving the amount of eye contact works well in large or small groups. Be careful that you don't focus on just one person in a group setting. Spread that eye contact around the room, and make those connections!

6

Breaking the Pattern
Business Complaints

Take a moment to critique your performance in most business situations. What are your biggest complaints? The importance of communicating with customers, partners, and coworkers is ever-present. This awareness can expose speech patterns that may be holding you back. There are reasons such patterns develop. Luckily, there are positive steps you can take to regain control and confidence.

I lose my train of thought!

What it feels like. Your train of thought is built on the concept of forward motion, just like a train. Losing your train of thought is a feeling of not being able to get any traction, like you keep starting and stopping.

It can feel like a need to fill up the pauses and open space or, to use a radio broadcasting term, "the dead air." You find yourself repeating the same phrase that always seems to fall flat. You feel as if you are continuously circling around the point of what you're trying to say with no direction. Sometimes you stumble, not being able to find the right words. There can be a sense of being on a road with no end. At the conclusion of many presentations or conversations you often realize, "That is *not* what I wanted to say!"

Why it happens. Losing your train of thought can be due to either a lack of good presentation preparation or a lack of confidence in your speech technique. When I say speech technique I am referring to the ability to think and speak at two different speeds. Many public speakers find themselves in a situation in which they're speaking too quickly. They often mistakenly determine that their minds can't keep up with their mouths. Actually the opposite is true. In the time it takes you to speak one simple thought, your mind is probably thinking five or six other thoughts, maybe more.

To further explain what is going on, we'll use the metaphor of conveyor belts in your mind. One belt that represents your speech is moving at a relatively slow and measured pace. The second conveyor belt moves along briskly; it represents the speed of the thoughts in your mind. The two can intersect smoothly only if you trust that they move at different speeds. Your mind shouldn't wait for your mouth and your mouth should never try to keep up with your mind.

Achieving the right balance involves trusting that the two conveyor belts can operate separately and simultaneously. Too much attention to your speech technique can make your words sound stiff and rehearsed. Trying to speak everything that's on your mind is to attempt the impossible, and is often the cause of getting off track.

A lack of forward momentum in your speech technique can also cause you to lose your way. Forward momentum begins in the body, not the mind. Disconnecting from the sense of speech being a full-body experience can begin to stifle your impulses that lead to supportive gesturing. This sends the message to your listeners, and the feedback to your mind, that you are not truly committed to what you're saying. The source of this disconnect is insufficient breathing.

Given enough time any individual can prepare for a big presentation. But it requires the right kind of preparation to make sure that your presentation grabs and holds your listener's attention. I have worked with many individuals who know the subject matter of their presentation backward and forward, but they often leave out the most important piece in their preparation. They forget to include their unique perspective.

What to do. Organizing and articulating your thoughts seem like very similar activities, yet a different set of skills is required for each. Having a firm grasp on the reason for needing to convey any message requires the use of a very important tool called the *bumper sticker*. The bumper sticker is a short phrase of only five or six words; short enough so that it will fit on a car bumper. It includes your unique understanding or perception of the material you are presenting. It requires asking yourself, "Why is this information important to me?" and "Why should it be important to my listeners?" Tapping into this visceral response to the material is the foundation for creating a truly compelling narrative. It isn't hard to revisit this concept during your speech and therefore emphasize your perspective because it includes how you feel about the subject at hand. It also shows a level of passion for what you're doing, a level of commitment that allows your listeners a framework within which they can decide for themselves how they feel about the topic and how they relate to it.

The next step to good presentation preparation is clearly defining the three most important ideas that brought you to your bumper sticker. Three ideas in any one sitting are pretty much any listener's limit. Don't get lost in the light show of information. Allow only one sentence for each reason. This will make the connection between how you feel about something and why you feel that way. Your presentation should always be about clarity of thought, forward momentum, and, ultimately, persuasion.

Deliberate breathing is the foundation for perception of commitment and forward momentum. If integrated correctly, it will also give you time to think and look as if you *are* thinking deliberately. The message you send by exposing your breathing is that you are truly considering your next words, that they are important to you. Try this breathing experiment.

Breathe deeply and hold your breath for one second. Then say, "I'm not sure we should try that today." Next, breathe deeply and hold your breath for two seconds before saying the same phrase. Follow that by breathing deeply for three seconds. This time allow your hands to gesture, emphasizing the same phrase. Finally, breathe deeply and hold your breath for four seconds, gesture, and notice how much you have increased the importance of what you're saying. You are now experiencing forward momentum and its connection to your body.

Use this breathing exercise on any bumper sticker of your choice. You will begin to feel the true meaning of the words in your gut. This is the visceral interpretation that will include your perspective. I cannot emphasize enough how essential this is to becoming a more focused and therefore a more compelling and persuasive speaker.

I never know when to jump in!

What it feels like. Never knowing when to jump in is a very common speech complaint. Whether you are in a business meeting, networking, or socializing, you have the same feeling of uncertainty; a feeling of being left behind. Adding to this is the voice in your head that reminds you that, "If you're going to speak up, you better make sure that you're right!" You begin to feel that what you have to say is an all-or-nothing proposition. There is a sense of building pressure because you know that you are expected to contribute, and even want to contribute, but you feel held back. This can be accompanied by the feeling that the right moment has passed you by. When an occasional opportunity does present itself, it can feel as if you're starting in neutral with no momentum. After the fact, you might even convince yourself that you're really just shy and not much of a talker.

Why it happens. The truth is that there never really is an exact right time to jump in, but there is an "as good as any" time. So, what is really holding you back? There are several mental and physical reasons for the uncertainty you feel. Most of the time it's a combination of both. On the body side we have unsupported speech, disconnect from your impulses, and a lack of receptive body language. On the mind side we have limited access to concise stories and that ever-present fear of not saying the right thing.

Deliberate diaphragmatic breathing is the means by which you support your speech. It allows you to feel connected to your impulses that lead to supportive gestures. Along with facial expressions, eye contact, and posture, these gestures make up what we call body language. There are studies that say that over 50 percent of a message is conveyed through body language. Therefore, even when you're not speaking there is a message being sent. A lack of awareness of the physical aspect of speech is what causes the constant need to get up to speed. Your motor should already be going!

Good mental preparation is as important as good physical preparation. Trying to come up with stories from your experience, on the spot, can be extremely daunting. Determining whether you're saying the right thing as you're saying it is also taking on some serious heavy lifting. If your body is at a standstill and your mind is worried and spinning, it's very hard to be comfortable with jumping in and speaking up.

What to do. You can prepare yourself to be better at jumping in during a meeting or in a conversation. Start by taking a long prep breath as if you are about to speak. Hold that breath for a moment, then exhale slowly. Continue to do this while making consistent eye contact with the speaker. This is what we mean by "getting your motor going." You will be sending a nonverbal message that you are following along with what they're say ing. You will also be convincing your mind and body that you are prepared to speak. Do not be surprised if the speaker pauses to invite your contribution simply based on his or her awareness of your deliberate breathing. You should always practice this kind of receptive body language.

The more expressive and nuanced body language that is used when actually speaking comes from being connected to your impulses. Connecting to your impulses once again requires connecting to the body with breath. The sensation that your speech is coming "from the gut" physically will open the door to how you feel about what you're saying. The end result is that you will gain access to the all-important visual aspect of speech. This will not only have an impact on your listeners but also it will send you feedback that you are "in the flow." You will greatly diminish the stifling feeling of being held back.

Next, you need to follow your curiosity. When you are wondering about something you are not as concerned with knowing exactly what it is. This approach will certainly lower the pressure of having to be right about everything. Curiosity comes across as authenticity, which is always welcome in a conversation or a meeting.

Remember that you have a license to retrace. Try using phrases like: "Going back to a point you made earlier, I'd like to add . . . " or "I know we touched on this earlier, but . . . " or "I have a quick question about what you said before."

Situations in which you are expected to jump in and contribute vary from conversations to meetings to networking events. These communication scenarios also vary in how long you have to prepare for them and their expected level of participation. In general, networking events demand a high level of participation but also allow for the most preparation. You should always prepare three stories from your life experience that describe you. That is correct. You need to prepare them. Consider the joyous times and the challenging times. These are the stories that matter to you. Whether you are talking about a vacation, a difficult work experience, or an individual who had an impact on you, make sure you explore how you feel about that story. Always include your perspective. It shows healthy self-respect and a willingness to share your genuine thoughts. Impress people with that!

Meetings also require an inclusion of your perspective to be successful. In preparing for a meeting, review how you came to understand the topic at hand. Then, describe what you know in one sentence. Meetings are not simply about storytelling. They are about being a concise storyteller. Your preparation and brevity will be appreciated. Remember that you can always elaborate upon request.

Simple conversations are usually much more spontaneous and reactionary. There is a natural rhythm of listening and speaking that is established between the participants. Relating your experience and your stories to the conversation is essential. Trust your intuition and your unique perspective, breathe deeply, and use body language to indicate that you would like to add something to the conversation. Knowing when to jump in is all about empowering your perspective and staying connected to your body. The key is to be fully prepared to do the "jumping."

I get intimidated by really good speakers!

What it feels like. Really good speakers are wonderful to listen to. However, being intimidated by their ability can make it very difficult to interact with them. You begin by comparing your voice to theirs and to the voices of other people in the room. You notice and begin to admire the confidence with which everybody else seems to communicate. You deem your thoughts and your perspective to be less important. You tell yourself that you really don't need to contribute.

When your obligation to speak is inevitable, you feel as if you don't deserve the sudden shift of attention toward you. On the other hand, you might be thinking that you want to avoid the deflated feeling that occurs when the energy of attention moves away from you and back to the lead speaker. You have the feeling that you need to do more to keep people's attention. You may even mistakenly believe that this is the time to start adding new words to your vocabulary, before you're even comfortable articulating them and using them in context.

You realize that speaking too little and speaking too much can both send a negative perception. Comparing yourself to a really good speaker can make it nearly impossible to achieve the elusive vocal balance that you need to succeed.

Why it happens. Vocal cords vary in size and thickness. Different shaped mouths and heads comprise the body's acoustic environment that makes each voice unique. People who speak well usually have developed good vocal balance. They use good breath support and have clear phonation with freely vibrating vocal folds. This gives them access to a larger percentage of their natural voice. To the listener, this correctly sounds like increased resonance and projection. To the speaker, the sensation of vocal balance leads to increased comfort and confidence. Couple that with clarity of thought and you have an individual who is a good speaker.

The feeling of intimidation is caused by a lack of awareness of the physiological and the psychological aspects of speech. Proper breathing and breath support, clear phonation, precise (yet relaxed) articulation, and supportive body language make up the basic physiological components. The basic psychological components are: a clear train of thought, perspectives, perceptions, and good preparation. Good speakers do and think many of these things naturally—lucky them! The good news for everyone else is that focusing on any of these speech components will have a positive ripple effect on all of the others.

If your thoughts aren't clear, you'll be less likely to want to put them out there. If you don't know how to put them out there, you'll worry and your thoughts won't be clear. This is the mind and body connection of speech.

What to do. Learn from a good speaker. Instead of worrying about keeping up, pay attention to the things they are doing well. Watch where they take their breaths. This may be difficult to detect as their breathing is so completely integrated into their communication style that it seems relaxed and effortless. They may use a combination of fast breaths that quicken the pace and more deliberate breaths that indicate thoughtfulness or gravitas regarding the things they say. Either way, the breathing is there, and they are using it.

Take notice of their hand gestures. They are definitive, supportive, and fluid. The seamless integration of gesturing requires holding one gesture until the impulse for the next gesture comes along. Supportive gestures are an indication that a speaker is connected to their body, their breathing, and their thoughts.

Become aware of the importance of eye contact. Good speakers follow the 80/50 rule. They look at you only 50 percent of the time when speaking but 80 percent of the time when listening. In larger groups they move their gaze around the room in an act of attention and inclusion.

Speakers that you admire are Masters of the Pause, and therefore masters of pacing. They know, either intuitively or by practice, that saying nothing can also send a message. People pay attention to what comes right after a well-timed pause.

Once you become aware of what a good speaker is really doing, try to emulate them. Integrate deliberate breathing into your communication style and feel the sensation of forward momentum. Tap into the impulses that lead to supportive gesturing. Use the proper amount of eye contact when speaking and listening with confidence. Understand the energy of attention that you will feel when speaking to a group or even one individual. Always include your perspective in all of your preparation. Maintain your curiosity about what others are saying and how you relate to it. Begin to trust your speech technique more and more as you recognize subtle improvements in your vocal balance.

When engaging with a good speaker, acknowledge the speaker's ability to convey a clear message and then suggest your additional perspective. People with good speech technique understand the importance of connecting with you. They tend to be very gracious because they are comfortable and confident in their ability to convey a clear and concise message.

A good speaker will welcome your perspective like a tennis player welcomes another player onto the court. They know that the joy is in the shared experience, not the winning. Anything else is doing it for the wrong reasons.

I never know what to do with my hands!

What it feels like. Feeling uncomfortable with your hands when speaking can be a big problem. Perhaps you have tried figuring out the right place to put your hands. You may have tried putting your hands in your pockets, or tried standing with arms locked down at your sides. You may keep your hands hidden behind your back. You may also have tried holding your hands together in front of you with fingers intertwined. These are a few of the most repeated static hand positions.

The constant thought that you need to be doing something with your hands while you're speaking can be overwhelming. Your words don't seem to flow the way you know they could or they should.

The thought may have crossed your mind that you don't want to move your hands around too much. So you choose to only move your hands on occasion, which then makes those isolated gestures feel heavy, and you feel very self-conscious about using them.

You may catch yourself repeating the same hand movement over and over again, sometimes without even being aware that you're doing it. You feel that as long as you have a clipboard, a podium, or note cards to hold onto you're safe. The truth is that you will probably look as if you're holding on for dear life. This misconception is right up there with calming your nerves by imagining the audience in their underwear. Who started that one?

You know that you need to do something to wake up the group, but you don't know how or even where the ability to do that comes from. You desperately want your gestures to flow and feel natural, not practiced. There is an undeniable feeling of being held back.

Why it happens. Moving your hands to convey a nonverbal message or in support of speech is referred to as gesturing. It is one aspect of body language. Body language accounts for more than half of how you convey a message. When you lack confidence in gesturing, you can only be half as effective as a storyteller.

You disconnect from your ability to use your hands properly when you disconnect from your impulses. The easiest way to find those impulses is through deliberate use of breath. So, breathing leads to impulses that lead to connected hand gestures.

Another reason for the disconnect may be poor preparation. In an attempt to make sure that you are gesturing appropriately, you may decide to practice in front of a mirror. The problem with using a mirror to practice is that you will create a visual connection that will not exist when it comes time to actually present. Connecting to your impulses that lead to creative and supportive gestures is visceral. It is certainly visual to your listeners, but not to you.

Some consideration also needs to be made regarding negative perceptions. Unintended messages can be sent by using the wrong body language. Always keeping your hands in your pockets can make you look guarded. Arms down at your sides might be perceived as rigidity. Placing your hands behind your back seems apologetic. Your hands clasped in front of you can make it look as if you're worried. Arms crossed might make you seem defiant. Constantly holding your palms up and out looks as if you're asking for acceptance. Touching your ears too often comes across as annoyance. The touching of the back of the neck is a behavioral sign of tension. Constant touching of the face is associated with nervousness. Repeatedly turning over one hand looks like lighthearted irreverence. Like a monotone voice, using the same gesture repeatedly can be misleading. You definitely run the risk of having your delivery seem flat and boring.

What to do. Gestures that come across as natural and spontaneous require a sense of balance that only comes from the mind trusting the body. So, how do you gain trust in something that you only do on occasion? You need to integrate breathing, following impulses, and gesturing into your everyday speech. The deliberate integration of breathing reconnects us and reminds us that speech is a full-body experience.

Begin by taking a deep breath, and then hold that breath for two seconds, allowing no air to escape. Use the air to speak the sentence "You're putting words in my mouth." Repeat these steps and the sentence, but this time gesture with both hands on *words*. Make sure you hold the gesture long after you finish speaking. Once again breathe deeply and change the spoken sentence to "That's not what I meant to say." Repeat this sentence and land a new gesture on the word *not*. Make sure you don't let go of the gesture. Now go back to speaking sentence one with a gesture; hold the gesture while you breathe deeply and then speak sentence two with a different gesture.

The smooth transition from one gesture to the next allows you to connect your ideas with body language. By holding a gesture until the impulse for the next gesture comes along, you no longer need to think about where to put your hands when speaking.

Gesturing is not only a requirement when addressing a large group, it is essential to all communication. Be aware of the need to adjust the scale of your gestures to fit the size of your audience and the tone of your message.

I hate public speaking!

What it feels like. I saved this one for last because I didn't want the concept of public speaking to be the first and only thing you focus on regarding your speech technique. What many individuals feel about public speaking is a combination of frustration, discomfort, and dread. Most people do not look forward to this opportunity to promote themselves and their ideas on the big stage. In fact, many fear what they expect they will feel.

Common feelings about public speaking can range from nervousness to negative thoughts. *Nerves* is the term we all use to describe the anticipation of something that we believe is going to happen. You know that all eyes will be on you. Along with that will come the sense of being judged. You may even blame yourself for agreeing to be hung out to dry in this way. This may lead to negative thoughts about the consequences of your actions both personally and professionally. Not only will you feel the frustration, but you'll feel the embarrassment too.

When you are actually participating in the act of public speaking, you may feel as if you need to take everyone's temperature in the room. In other words, you mistakenly try to determine what your listeners are thinking while you are speaking. Talk about stacking the deck! You find yourself waiting for a response from your listeners to validate whether or not you're getting your point across. The waiting and watching distracts you, and you begin to lose your train of thought. The sense of obligation to keep their attention begins to grow. You feel as if you need to energize your presentation by picking up your pace. Then you realize that you don't know how to slow down. Finally, you just want to get the experience over with as quickly as possible. You feel as if you are on display and there is nowhere to run and hide from your inability and fear.

Why it happens. Public speaking has heightened physiological and psychological aspects to it. You really do need to use your body to project more and to slow your pace to make sure you are getting your point across. There is also a lot to consider and prepare for mentally.

The first step toward understanding why we dislike public speaking so much is to become aware of the energy of attention. Even in a one-on-one conversation you can feel the energy of another individual's attention being directed toward you. Imagine, or rather, predict what that energy might feel like if ten or more people turn their attention your way. That would be ten times the energy and attention being directed right at you. The energy is real. To believe that you can avoid this energy is to believe that you can do the impossible. Putting yourself in this position will always cause a feeling of discomfort that can lead to a fight-or-flight response. Your breathing rate and your heart rate both begin to increase. This physical response can cause you to lose focus on your breathing, and it becomes shallow. Insufficient breathing leads to a lack of projection and an uncontrollable increase in your rate of speech.

Next, you need to understand that effective public speaking has a lot to do with preparation. Insufficient preparation is mostly due to a lack of clarity or overstuffing. Failure to include your perspective leads to the need to include more and more information. Most listeners can only absorb three concepts at a time, provided that the concepts are connected by a common thread. Any more than that and you really are running the risk of losing them.

The last part of the public speaking mystery lies in the body. Thinking that the fear and the feelings are all in your head can make you forget how physical the act of speech truly is. If your body, your breathing, and your body language are not all there in support of what you're saying, your message will fall flat, and you will know it!

What to do. Fearing the energy of attention can be put into perspective by using the analogy of standing at the edge of a lake and asking yourself, "When I jump in this lake, will I or won't I get wet?" Worrying about whether you'll get wet or not is silly. You know it's going to happen. The sensation of all eyes being on you when you get up to speak is a reality too. Learning how to deal with the reality of jumping in the lake is what we call *habituating with a circumstance.* In other words, you have to learn to get used to it. Certainly jumping in the lake carries with it more danger than getting up in front of a group of individuals, but we decide to live with that danger and jump in anyway. If you decide to jump in the lake, yet you don't trust your swimming technique when you do it, you're truly putting yourself in a compromised position. Swimming is something that most of us don't do on a daily basis, just like public speaking. You need to move toward building your speech technique and trusting it—not running away from it.

When your thought process is clouded by worry, you need to go back to your body for some sense of control. You need to practice controlled breathing. In preparation for a big speech or presentation, most people will tell you to take a deep breath to calm down. I want to take it a step further. Take a deep breath, hold that breath for a moment, and recognize that you own it. Then make a buzzing sound like a bee with a voiced Z for a minimum of ten seconds. Repeat this several times until you feel reconnected to your breathing. If the nerves hit you during your speech, follow the same steps but replace the buzzing sound with the words you want to speak.

The breathing muscle in your body, your diaphragm, is responsible for the forward momentum of your speech. It also serves as your brakes to slow you down. The more you practice starting and stopping using your diaphragm, the more comfortable you will be with pausing and changing speech rhythm. Pausing allows you the time you need to take another deliberate breath. It also helps keep your pace from escalating out of control while giving your listeners a moment to process what you have just said.

The clarity you need to comfortably convey a compelling message comes from your ability to distill all of the information down to a single bumper sticker. This is a short phrase that includes why you need to say what you're saying. It is not simply the obligation that you have to speak but the reason why it is important to you. Speak this several times with good breath support and a gesture that makes your body feel included in the discovery. It may not happen right away, but it is well worth the effort. You will be training your mind and your body to work together, giving you the confidence that you won't lose your train of thought. A bumper sticker is that thought that you can hold onto and build upon during your speech. Determine the three most important concepts that support your bumper sticker, and you will have clarity. Remember that effective public speaking requires inward grounding. The outward expression can only be built on clarity of thought and the support of the body.

7

Breathing with Authority
Powerful Speech Techniques

A very common goal in business is to develop a more authoritative voice. In order to speak with authority, you first have to consistently breathe with authority. Most people just don't breathe very well. They don't realize that their breath is their vocal fuel. It seems pretty obvious that you need more breath when trying to speak louder, but good breath support helps eliminate so many other vocal problems too. It is the key to relaxing your voice so it can sound confident, poised, and authoritative. Whenever I offer a speech client the simple advice to "make sure you breathe," I can see that look in their eyes. I imagine them wanting to say, "Are you kidding me? That's something I do automatically!" That's true. It is also true that if they passed out from public-speaking anxiety, they would continue to breathe involuntarily too. There is breathing automatically, and then there's breathing effectively. In both obvious and subtle ways breath support and well-timed breathing increase your ability to communicate with authority and presence.

Sneak a breath. Let's start with the understanding that it's okay to show that you are, in fact, breathing. People often convince themselves that they should "catch a breath" under their listener's radar. They mistakenly believe that allowing anyone to see you breathe will make you seem nervous and unprepared. The exact opposite projection is absolutely true. Take a deep breath and hold that breath for a second, then say, "I will find a way to make this work." Think about the various perceptions an empathetic listener could have from hearing the delivery of these words. They might think of you as being determined, resolute, trustworthy, and mature. These are all wonderfully descriptive adjectives for anyone who wants to be a successful business and personal communicator. It truly falls under the category of "it's not what you say, but how you say it."

Exercises for breath integration. Take a deep breath through your nose and hold it, then exhale slowly. Now try taking a quick inhalation through your mouth and holding it. Exhale slowly again. You now know how to take a quick breath and how to take a slow and more deliberate breath. Of course, deliberate breath integration means using your breaths, slow or fast, as part of your everyday communication style. Let's add words to the mix. Take a deep breath through your nose once again and speak slowly, saying,

"We need a better strategy for completing phase one of the project . . . "

(Take a quick mouth breath and say), " . . . and we need it by Tuesday."

Allow your gestures and your facial expressions to go right along with your emphatic exhalation. Once again, let yourself go rather than hold yourself back. Gesture fully, completely, and even wildly, if you like. You can always rein it in when speaking with others.

At first, it may feel as if you're hanging on every word, like you're attempting a bad impersonation of Marlon Brando in *A Streetcar Named Desire.* Don't give up! You have to stay disciplined to effect any kind of change. Don't speed up either your breathing or your speech pace when practicing breath integration. You can expect to slowly gain comfort and confidence in relying on your newfound breath support.

Baby's belly. The diaphragm is the primary muscle used in the process of respiration. It separates your chest cavity from your abdomen. The diaphragm muscle is responsible for regulating the air that goes into and out of the lungs. There is no vocal sound without the exhalation of air; there is no exhalation without first having inhalation. Both are controlled by the diaphragm muscle. It is the largest muscle in your vocal apparatus and often the most neglected.

Have you ever seen a video of a baby or a dog sleeping on YouTube? You can see their belly going out and in, out and in. Their chest and shoulders remain relaxed and calm. This is also the way <u>we</u> are supposed to breathe naturally and in a relaxed manner. The belly moving out and in is an indication that the diaphragm muscle is working properly. As air comes into the lungs, they fill up and the diaphragm muscle pushes down on the abdomen. Since the diaphragm muscle is right in between your chest cavity, which houses your lungs and your abdomen, it has to make room for the lungs to expand, therefore pushing down on your belly. This is the outward indication that you are breathing properly. Do not allow your shoulders or chest to rise dramatically when breathing. This will cause the diaphragm muscle to rise and will decrease the amount of space you have to take in a sufficient breath of air. Learn to breathe correctly all the time, not only when you're speaking.

Exercises for diaphragm recognition. It is very important that you recognize the sensation of using your diaphragm muscle. It is the engine that drives all speech. Try breathing normally, and count the seconds it takes for you to inhale and then exhale. Both should average about two seconds. Now, breathe deeply from the belly. The time it takes to inhale and exhale will increase by as much as two seconds to about four seconds.

Next, inhale deeply again for four seconds, open your mouth as if you are being examined by the dentist, and say, "ah." Continue saying "ah" for twelve seconds. Why are we able to extend our exhalation for so much longer when voicing sound? The answer has to do with resistance and diaphragm regulation. It probably seems pretty obvious that if your air stream has to pass through and vibrate your vocal cords it will slow down. The active regulation of your diaphragm has a lot to do with it, too.

Breathe deeply one more time. Then, attempt to exhale for twelve seconds without voicing a sound. You will notice that, in order to extend your exhale, you will need to hold back the air using just your diaphragm. You will definitely feel this muscle at work. Diaphragm regulation isn't easy at first, but you can teach yourself to master it over time.

Barely breathing. The majority of speech clients focus on everything but breathing. For some, the focus is articulation, or organizing their thoughts, or where to put their hands. The reason for this is because they have already figured out a way to communicate while barely breathing at all! This is certainly not the best way to do it. You have created a behavioral pattern requiring that you compensate to make up for a lack of efficient breathing. Without good breath support your articulators and your jaw will become more tense. The muscles surrounding your larynx and vocal cords may start to help out in ways that eventually will hold your voice back. Most individuals mistakenly think that their minds are holding them back. In reality, they are reacting to the sensations caused by inefficient breathing for speech. Changing the way that you speak for the better requires changing behavior. It requires the discipline to change at a very fundamental level.

Exercises for breath preparation. Good breathing simply does not get enough credit. Take a moment to explore you own abilities with a little experiment. Take a deep breath, pause for a beat, then deliver the following phrase, emphasizing the word *got.*

"You've got to be kidding!"

It should feel as if the words are coming from your core or "from your gut." That is a great place to draw from physically, spiritually, and creatively. There are many benefits to approaching breathing and speech in this way. The obvious benefit is that your voice feels "fueled" and sounds more resonant. The subtle benefit is the outward perception that you are passionate, in control, and truly speak from the heart.

Put the emphasis on the word *I* in this next sentence:

"I will look into it personally."

Your new focus on breathing may bring about some other unexpected behavioral changes. You will probably find yourself yawning more than ever before. This occurs because you are breathing more consistently and your body likes it. Increased oxygen intake improves physical and mental functions. Yawning also causes your larynx, which houses your vocal chords, to lower involuntarily to a more relaxed position. Yawning is a very good thing when you are doing your speech exercises. Don't stifle it; go with it!

Strange rhymes with *change.* Let's take a moment to talk about how strange these adjustments to your breathing are going to feel. Since breath support is the basis for all good speech, you'll certainly have the feeling that you are rocking your foundation. Let me remind you that *strange* rhymes with *change,* and you can't really have one without the other. Stay the course through the uncomfortable adjustment. The sudden access and integration of a substantially larger amount of breath may leave you feeling light-headed and overstuffed with air. You may even feel as if you're being awkwardly obvious in your breathing. Remember that there are positive perceptions to be projected by approaching your breathing in this way. You probably have never even considered them before. Deliberate breathing needs to become one of the most important tools you can use to take your communication ability to the next level.

Exercises for accessing breath with comfort. It may seem strange to know that in order to increase your comfort with accessing breath, you're going to have to push yourself. Your body and your mind have already developed a pattern of speech that has worked fairly well up until now. Trust me when I say that your foundation needs to be stronger. Use this exercise that integrates breathing, eye contact, and gesturing to convince both your body and your mind that deliberate breathing works.

Pick a spot on the wall and designate it as the place where you make direct eye contact with your listener. Move your gaze a few inches away from that spot and take a slow, deliberate breath. As you inhale slowly, raise both of your hands, keeping your elbows by your side. Hold your breath for a moment. Look back at your listener and slowly speak the words,

"I don't think I really understand what you mean."

Allow your hands to fall just a few inches on the word *don't*, therefore emphasizing the word with body language. Repeat this exercise until you begin to synchronize your breathing, the changing of your eye contact, and your gesturing. It may seem as if you are being asked to do quite a few things all at once, but inevitably all of these elements of speech will need to be connected to each other. The end result of this repetition will be an increased feeling of support and comfort.

Vocal fuel. Your breath is your vocal fuel. Used properly it can bring so many wonderful qualities to your speech technique. When you need to project, your breath is your rocket fuel. When you need to get your point across, your breath is your forward momentum. When you are speaking intimately, it is the resonance that makes your voice warm and inviting. You always want to make sure you have enough fuel in the tank to say the things you want to say with authority. You don't want to use up all of your fuel right in the beginning of a sentence. You want to make sure you have enough stored up to finish your spoken ideas definitively. If you feel yourself running out of air, you have to know it's okay to take another breath, no matter where in the sentence that breath may be required. The key is to stay supported.

Exercises for recognizing good breath support. Staying well supported means always speaking on breath. Don't think of breath support as being something you establish only at the beginning of the sentence. You may find yourself needing to breathe in unexpected places. Give yourself permission to do it. Speaking on breath means never allowing yourself to speak in an unsupported way.

Try speaking the following sentences, taking a deep breath at the beginning of each sentence and then midsentence where indicated:

"I thought I knew everything about the subject" (deep breath), "but now I'm not so sure."

"You could have told me sooner" (deep breath), "but thank you for telling me."

"We reached out to a number of volunteers." (deep breath) "None were available."

By integrating more frequent breaths, you will remove the temptation to speed up your sentences in order to fit everything in on one single breath. An additional bonus is that you will not only sound more grounded in your speech but will also feel more grounded. You will feel less rushed.

Good breath support is essential to increasing your comfort with the idea of exploring pitch variation, both high and low. Limiting your breath support means limiting your ability to step out of a very narrow comfort zone. A very narrow zone of speech is referred to as a monotone. This voice varies very little in pitch and rhythm.

Ration it out. To effectively breathe with authority, you need to focus on regulating your diaphragm muscle. You need to be in charge of how quickly you let the air out of your lungs. Whether you are projecting your voice or speaking at a normal level, you need to recognize the balance required to make sure that your voice is always well supported. Pushing too much air at the beginning of speech is what we call "bursting." It puts undue stress on your vocal cords and the muscles surrounding your vocal cords and dissipates your vocal fuel much too quickly. You control the rate at which the air is pushed out of your lungs by using your diaphragm muscle. This is the foundation upon which your speech technique is built.

Exercises for diaphragm strengthening. Breathe in as you would normally for a second or two, and then breathe out for a second or two. Repeat this deliberate action two or three times. Then inhale for two seconds and exhale all of your air in two seconds while saying the words,

"Where do you want to go today?"

Speaking these words completely on a normal exhale will probably sound very rushed to your ears. Now inhale for two seconds and speak those same words at a more measured and regular-sounding pace. It will probably take you about four seconds to complete speaking the sentence and expel the air from your lungs.

Now try speaking the same sentence, pausing at each ellipses for a full second, without taking an additional breath.

"Where . . . do you want . . . to go . . . today?"

This is how you control your rate of speech by using your diaphragm muscle. (In later chapters, we will explore how to affect your rate of speech using elongated articulation.) Remember, when you hold it, you own it.

Speaking in waves. We don't just think ideas and then speak them. Your mind gives you the impulse to speak, which sends a signal down to your diaphragm muscle, and it is this muscle that starts and stops your spoken words. Your diaphragm is in control of the rhythm, or cadence, of your speech. There will certainly be times when stopping and starting your speech can be used for emphasis, but for the most part you want your words to flow. Therefore, you need to understand how to speak on breath—in other words, how to use your breath to allow your words to flow.

Good speech rhythm that flows easily does not mean speaking quickly; it does mean understanding that for the most part we speak in waves. Just like the waves in the ocean, your speech patterns have peaks and valleys or crests and troughs. Think of the crest of the wave as being the point at which you take your supportive breath. You begin to speak and start heading down the wave into the trough only to rise back up to the crest in time to take another breath. You need to be connected to your breath in order to execute this effective and dynamic pattern of speech.

Exercises for breathing in rhythm. Speaking in waves is wonderfully effective, but overusing this technique can lead to a speech pattern that is much too "sing-song." You need to break it up by varying rhythm consistently. When you focus on your breathing, you can develop the ability to slow down the pace of your speech. Far too often, a sense of lacking enough air to finish a sentence or phrase will cause a speaker to start to speed up and eventually start rolling out of control. Breathing will give you the support necessary to end your sentences with authority. Take a deep breath, pause, and say,

"Everyone in attendance truly . . . learned . . . a lot."

Landing the last word of any sentence or phrase in a declarative manner with separation between the words requires sufficient breath support—especially when the last word has a large, wide-open vowel like the *ah* sound in *lot*.

Now try reversing rhythm by stopping in the beginning of this sentence and flowing through the second half.

"There . . . are . . . several different ways we can look at this."

Notice that every time you stop your speech you can feel a slight pull in your diaphragm muscle. Stopping the air means stopping the sound. Remember to only start to sound again when you are quite sure you have enough air to do it. If not, simply take another breath.

Simple complexity. We are all empathetic listeners. We all want to relate to and connect with shared ideas. Good breathing and breath support slows down the exchange of ideas to allow for a real connection. By speaking with authority we are communicating that the words we are saying are important to us, and consequently, that the words should be important to the listener. This means that we understand the importance of the listener. We all do like to feel important!

The approach to speaking well is very basic, but the perceptions that the approach can convey are very intriguing. The positive perceptions that good, deliberate breathing can convey range from having forward momentum to relaxation, comfort, and confidence. When integrated consistently into your everyday communications, good breathing can be the silent continuity between your spoken ideas. It is the foundation for every improvement you can make to your speaking style.

Exercises for projecting positive perceptions. Like it or not, you have to be very deliberate when practicing breathing exercises. What feels extreme in practice will become tempered when you use your new techniques for everyday speech. Try this exercise to add a sense of gravitas, or weight, to your words. Inhale slowly through your nose; hold your breath for a second. Tilt your head and gesture as you say this sentence:

"Which of these topics *is* a priority?"

Repeat this sentence, extending the amount of time that you hold your breath before speaking to two seconds, and then to three seconds. You will definitely feel the effect that breathing has on the message you are conveying. Your question will increase in urgency. Any listener would determine that your words are considered and sincere. This is a wonderful example of the charismatic appeal of speaking with thoughtfulness and dignity.

Take the focus on your breath support a step further and make your breathing a part of your creative interpretation. Repeat the same preparation steps as before. This time while you were pausing to hold your breath, smile broadly and say,

"I never thought of it that way."

Obviously, what you are doing is adding layers to a strong foundation of breathing and breath support. The not-so-obvious point is that none of it will work without the breathing. You will also discover a deeper connection to your impulses, thoughts, and motivations through good breath support. Breath is your vocal relaxer, which will increase your comfort and ultimately, your confidence.

8

No Shouting Please
Controlled Speech Techniques

Once you accept the importance of breathing you need to know where to put all of that good breath. Speaking up in a business meeting can sound like shouting if you just take a deep breath and go for it. Necessary vocal balance can only be achieved by becoming more vowel centric. The process begins with the recognition of the long and short vowels in American English. Discovering the sensation of speaking words with the lower, elongated vowel sounds: *aa*, *ah*, *au*, and *oh*, along with vowel combinations, leads to more wide open and relaxed phonation. Repetitive vowel exercises will ultimately increase vowel space, resonance, projection, and, most importantly, relaxation.

Gut check. The sound of shouting is the sound of tension. You certainly recognize it when you hear it. Though you may feel tense at times, that is certainly not the perception you want to project when speaking. So, in order to feel more relaxed, you need to develop a technique that will reduce the tension in your voice. Any good technique is built on fundamentals. You can physically control the amount of tension in your voice with your breathing. For most, step number one is recognizing the diaphragm muscle. You need to know where it is, what it is, and how to regulate it. You might think of a gut check as being something you do during a time of stress or tension. The truth is, if you're not breathing in a relaxed way, every time you speak you are experiencing a certain amount of tension. Remember, relaxation leads to comfort, which leads to confidence. There are no shortcuts.

Exercises for diaphragm recognition. Take a moment to become aware of your breathing. Feel the expansion of your abdomen and sides as you breathe in. Keep your shoulders and chest relaxed with each breath. Your focus should be on your abdomen, which contains the breathing muscle calling the diaphragm. Your diaphragm's sole purpose is to rise and fall, moving air in and out of your lungs. When you breathe in, your lungs expand and your belly goes out. As you breathe out, your belly pushes in and up on your lungs, moving the air upward. This may seem a little confusing at first: breath in—belly out, breath out—belly in. But you will get the hang of it. I cannot stress the importance of relaxed and deliberate breathing enough. Don't move on until you become comfortable with this manner of breathing. It is the foundation for everything else to come.

Low is the way to go. Good vocal space is not just a matter of dropping your jaw and opening your mouth wider, although this will certainly help to an extent. The real challenge is in learning to allow your voice to exist in a bigger space. Ultimately, allowing your voice to live in a bigger space, created by lowering your larynx with good breath support, will increase your confidence and improve your overall presentation and communication skills. To achieve this, you must learn how to properly support your voice, how to make sounds using that support, and how to break the habits that hold back your voice.

Exercises for vocal relaxation. For better or worse, we use our voices everyday. This accounts for why it can be so hard to get rid of old, inefficient habits. The mental and physical pressures of each day have a direct impact on the larynx and vocal cords, too. The two biggest factors that put strain on the larynx, and cause it to rise, are feeling stressed and being tired. It often feels as if these two factors are a constant. Therefore, learning how to relax your voice is crucial to vocal survival.

Here is a daily relaxation exercise to explore. Yawn. That's right. As stressed and tired as you feel everyday, it should be easy. Start by forcing yourself to yawn. Then, it should be hard to stop. Good! Yawning is very good for your voice. The larynx involuntarily lowers with each yawn. A lowered larynx is a larynx in its most relaxed position. Yawn again. Now try speaking at a normal volume and at a deliberate pace. The ease of speech might only last a few seconds, but it does feel good!

Yawning is not the only way to reduce tension in your voice. Here is a simple daily exercise that can have profound results. Take a long, relaxed inhalation of breath, and hold your breath for a second as you open your mouth as if you were being examined by the doctor or the dentist. Keep your mouth in that open position and say "ah" for five or six seconds. Avoid the temptation to look up at the ceiling or allow your mouth to slowly close as you're making this sound. Don't let your volume get too loud or too soft. Keep it consistent. Repeat this exercise for three to four minutes as you feel the tension in the throat muscles surrounding your larynx reduce.

You can increase the vocal space and relaxation even more by repeating this exercise with a slight tongue adjustment. Try placing the tip of your tongue in front of your bottom teeth and behind your lower lip. Take a relaxed breath like before, hold that breath for a second, and open your mouth as if being examined. Once again make the sound "ah" for five or six seconds. You will probably feel an urge to pull your tongue back in your mouth. Make sure you hold the tip of your tongue in this position. It may take a moment or two to be comfortable with your tongue in this position. Ultimately, it will give you more vocal space and vocal relaxation.

A relaxed voice does not mean a dull, boring monotone. On the contrary, relaxation allows for a feeling of ease in the speaker and the perception of ease by the listener. To the listener it sounds as if an individual is speaking their mind because the spoken ideas truly are flowing out on a breath of air.

Look behind you. Once you've built the foundation for your voice, you can begin to refine the sounds you make. Many individuals searching for improved speech will mistakenly put too much focus on consonant articulation. They are looking in the wrong direction. They need to turn around and focus on the vowels. The true path to a bigger and better voice lies in awareness of vowel placement. You need to know where the different vowel sounds resonate in your mouth and make sure you place them where they need to go, with good breath support. Luckily, not all vowels have the same breath support obligation. You don't need to focus on them all, but you do need to know the differences between them.

Exercises for proper vowel placement. There are twelve different vowel positions. The front vowels are probably the easiest to recognize. They are (from highest to lowest): *ee* as in "beet," *ih* as in "bit," *ay*" as in "bait," *eh* as in "bet," and *aa* as in "bat." Try speaking each "as in" word twice in a row:

"Beet, beet, bit, bit, bait, bait, bet, bet, bat, bat."

You should feel a need to open your mouth as you go to increase the space necessary for creating each lower vowel.

The next set of middle vowels are a little harder to recognize: *er* as in "Bert," *uh* as in "but," and once again, the lowest vowel, *ah* as in "Bob." Try speaking each of these "as in" words twice in a row:

"Bert, Bert, but, but, Bob, Bob."

You should feel a middle-of-the-mouth sensation, approximately where your hard palate and soft palate meet. Watch out for any sensation of gripping in the cheek muscles. This should be avoided.

Most people have trouble properly placing one or more of the back vowels: long *oo* as in "boot," short *oo* as in "book," long *oh* as in "boat," and *aw* as in "ball." Try speaking each of these "as in" words twice in a row:

"Boot, boot, book, book, boat, boat, ball, ball."

You should feel a back-of-the-mouth sensation in the area of your soft palate. It can be described as a domed feeling. There is a tendency for the mind to see any *oo* word and think of the ghostly *boo* sound with lips pushed forward. This will force your sound forward where it will be robbed of vitality and clarity. Just allow it to live in the back of the mouth.

Length matters. It is important to recognize that some vowel sounds in American English are very long and some are very short. There are no vowel sounds that are in between. Short vowel sounds are very clipped, and long vowels sounds require that you linger a little longer when making the sound. Very few speakers would ever try to make a short vowel very long, but many speakers don't give their long vowel sounds enough space in their mouths.

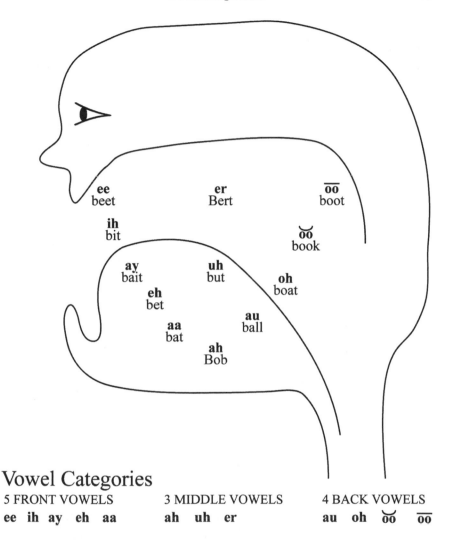

Vowel Categories

5 FRONT VOWELS	3 MIDDLE VOWELS	4 BACK VOWELS
ee ih ay eh aa	**ah uh er**	**au oh o͝o o͞o**

Exercises for recognizing long and short vowels. It is essential that you know the difference between your long and short vowel sounds. Here are fifty (or so) single-syllable words that are designated as being either long or short based on the length of the vowel.

Words with Short Vowels
in let her love book it yet turn up should ill get
girl chuck look foot cut good some first sing young
wood

Words with Long Vowels
go   ball   sock   bait   need   food   bags   we   face   bad   not
true   own   call   track   shoe   door   home   meet   she   sail   hot
had   base   soup   store boat

Here are those same words put into long and short vowel word combinations. Notice that when a word has a short vowel sound in American English it is very short and clipped. Words with long vowel sounds require
more breath and time to speak correctly. This is a key to developing a
more relaxed sound. Your voice will sound more relaxed to your listeners
because you will be feeling more relaxed. Take your time with the long
vowel sounds.

1: First Word Short/Second Word Long
   let go, foot ball, her sock, cut bait, in need, good food, some bags

2: First Word Long/Second Word Short
   we should, face book, bad turn, not yet, true love, own it, call up

3: First Word Long/Second Word Long
   track meet, shoe store, door knob, home base, she had, sail boat, hot
   soup

4: First Word Short/Second Word Short
   first look, sing well, get ill, young girl, wood chuck

Splitting hairs. There are many differing opinions about what is a true
vowel sound and what is a combination of vowel sounds called a diphthong. The only thing you really need to pay attention to is large vowel
sounds, whether they are primary vowel sounds or diphthongs. Large
vowel sounds are long and resonate lower in your mouth. These big
vowel sounds should be your primary focus to get the fastest results.
When properly supported with breath, they add resonance to your voice,
along with the ability to project and the opportunity to relax your larynx
and vocal cords.

   Exercises for recognizing the largest vowel sounds. Large vowel sounds
can either be a single vowel or combinations of two or three vowels. The
largest and most often used vowel sounds in American English are:

aa (as in *cat*), *ah* (as in *got*), *au* (as in *call*), *oh* (as in *snow*)
ah-ee (as *in my*), *aa-oo* (as *in out*), *au-ee* (as *in boy*)
eh-er (as in *air*), *au-er* (as in *store*)
aa-er (as in *are*), *oo-er* (as in *fewer*), *ee-er* (as in *here*)
aa-ee-er (as in *fire*), *aa-oo-er* (as in *power*), and *au-ee-er* (as in *lawyer*)

Notice that the *r* is considered a vowel sound in the phonetics world because the sound is made with an unobstructed, or open, vocal tract.

No short changing! They say the best diets are lifestyle changes. Yes, you will feel better and look better if you can maintain a healthy diet. Consider maintaining vowel space to be like a diet. For so many, this is a completely different way of looking at speech. But it will make you sound better and feel better. Good vocal balance is achieved by focusing on the vowels and being consistent. When you're feeling tired and unfocused is when your vowels suffer the most. You don't have to worry about short vowels because they're easy to speak. The long vowels need your focus and breath support. Don't shortchange your relaxation, your projection, and your resonance.

Exercises for maintaining vowel space. If you have been consistently speaking with very little breath support, we have already made some physical adjustments that will need to be corrected. This correction will feel strange when you first attempt it. Remember that change can only occur through awareness, acceptance, and action. Now that you are aware of the existence of large vowels, you need to accept an adjustment to your usual manner of speaking. Repeating the following exercise is the action required to gain better vowel space.

Say each one of the "as in" words from the previous exercise, and then speak the two additional words that rhyme and contain the same vowel sound. Make sure you take your time and speak each word slowly. They all contain large vowel sounds that need good vowel space and support.

cat - that - sat   got - not - pot
call - wall - tall   snow - blow - go
my - guy - lie   out - shout - pout
boy - toy - coy   air - bear - there
store - more - for   are - car - far
poor - doer - fewer   here - near - steer
fire - tire - buyer   flower - power - hour
lawyer - foyer - destroyer

Ah, yes! Focusing on the vowels is enormously beneficial to improving your speech technique. The first benefit is that you will be able to project your voice. Creating a larger and more relaxed space in your mouth for these large vowel sounds means you are creating a larger acoustic space. Second, the increased relaxation that comes with well-supported vowel sounds will make you feel more relaxed. The third benefit is that you will have access to a larger percentage of your natural voice. This is what we mean by increasing voice resonance. Treating vowels as small things leads to having a small voice. Speaking large vowels with appropriate space and good breath support leads to a more resonant and warmer voice.

There may be times during your practice when you wonder whether you're doing it right. Keep in mind that it's important to focus on how these sounds feel rather than how you hear them. We are all constantly monitoring our own speech; we know what we like and what doesn't sound good to our ears, even though we cannot hear ourselves the way the rest of the world hears us. Thus, trying to "help" your voice sound better to you can lead to detrimental vocal habits, such as squeezing the throat, widening the mouth horizontally, clenching the tongue, and tightening of the jaw (to name just a few), all of which destroy the relaxed, resonant space you are working to create. These bad habits can be hard to detect on your own, but some of the inevitable symptoms are vocal fatigue, muscle strain, and a diminished or choked sound.

Exercises for increasing voice resonance. Now that you know that focusing on the vowels is the way to warm up the tone of your voice, try speaking the following sentences, focusing on where those large vowels exist. This is how you can add weight, or gravitas, to your voice while still staying relaxed, comfortable, and confident sounding. Make sure you take a nice, deliberate breath before speaking each sentence.

"Good morning, ladies and gentlemen."

The large vowels are: the *au-er* sound of *morning*, the long *ai* sound of *ladies*, the *aa* sound of *and*. The rest are all short.

"What factors are driving this trend?"

The large vowels are: the *aa* sound of *factor*, the *ah-er* sound of *are*, the *ah-ee* sound of *driving*. The rest are all short.

"I will ask the members of the board tomorrow."

The large vowels are: the *ah-ee* sound of *I*, the *aa* sound of *ask*, the *au-er* sound of *board*, the *ah* sound of *tomorrow*. The rest are all short.

"There's nothing more to discuss."

The large vowels are: the *eh-er* sound of *there's*, the *au-er* sound of *more*. The rest are all short.

"That idea is not in keeping with company policy."

The large vowels are: the *aa* sound of *that*, the *ah-ee* sound of *idea* as well as the *ee* into *ah* sound of *idea*, the *ah* sound of *not*, the *ah* sound of *policy*. The rest are all short.

Noisy is as noisy does. Noisy environments can wreak havoc on anyone's voice. It is important to stay balanced and well supported where talking, sound, or music is polluting the environment. Noisy restaurants, busy city streets, loud nightclubs, and music concerts are very hard to compete with. Try to limit speaking in these situations as much as possible, but when you have to communicate make sure you use deliberate breathing, and open your mouth to create and maintain really good vowel space. Keep your phrases short and well supported with your breath, and let your gestures and facial expressions help you get your message across. Try to avoid grinding your voice or pushing it beyond its limits.

Exercises for relaxed projection. Use a similar approach to projecting your voice as you would for increasing the resonance of your voice. Focus on the large vowel sounds in the sentences that you speak. They are all long vowels, and they also resonate lower in your mouth. These are the sounds that require you to open your mouth and relax your jaw. They have the most acoustic space and create the biggest sound.

Say the phrase: "Not on my watch!"

Recognize that every vowel sound is long and low in this phrase. There are no short vowels. Say the phrase again slowly, with a relaxed jaw, and focus on each large vowel. You should experience an increase in your volume and ability to project.

Say the sentence, "I had a long day at the office."

Recognize the large, low vowel space in the words *I*, *had*, *long*, *at*, and *office*. The rest of the vowels are short. Say the sentence again, this time focusing on the vowel space of *I*, *had*, *long*, *at*, and *office*. You should experience an increase in your volume and ability to project.

Say the sentence, "We'd like to begin the meeting now."

Recognize the large, low vowel space in the words *like* and *now*. *We'd* and *meeting* have long vowels, but they are not low. The rest of the vowels are short. Say the sentence again, this time focusing on the vowel space of *like* and *now*. You should experience an increase in your volume and ability to project.

Say the sentence, "Where does the bus stop?"

Recognize the large, low vowel space in the words *Where* and *stop*. The rest of the vowels are short. Say the sentence again, this time focusing on the vowel space of *Where* and *stop*. You should experience an increase in your volume and ability to project.

Say the sentence, "This song is one of my favorites."

Recognize the large, low vowel space in the words *song* and *my*. *Favorites* has a long vowel, but it is not low. The rest of the vowels are short. Say the sentence again, this time focusing on the vowel space of *song* and *my*. You should experience an increase in your volume and ability to project.

Say the sentence, "It's really crowded tonight!"

Recognize the large, low vowel space in the words *crowded* and *tonight* (second syllable). *Really* has long vowels, but it is not low. The rest of the vowels are short. Say the sentence again, this time focusing on the vowel space of *crowded* and *tonight* (second syllable). You should experience an increase in your volume and ability to project.

A full, confident voice is free of constriction. Focusing on the large vowels and flowing on breath are essential to improving the overall tone of your voice. This approach will also make it easier for you to speak up without sounding as if you need to shout it out!

9

Those Sneaky Leaks
Clear Speech Techniques

The feeling of being out of breath when speaking is often due to air leakage. You may have developed the habit of starting to speak with too little air in your lungs. Pushing too much air at the start of a sentence and then trailing off is a common speech habit referred to as "bursting." The muscles in the throat surrounding the larynx and vocal cords will always compensate for a lack of balanced breath support. The overarticulation of certain consonant sounds can also be the primary cause of leakage. Recognizing the difference between voiceless and voiced consonant sounds is crucial to gaining more efficient use of your breath. The mouth and lips can also be affected adversely by overarticulation. The execution of precise, yet relaxed, articulation exudes a sense of comfort and projects confidence to your listeners.

We speak on breath; that means having a sense of vocal balance. Anything that upsets that balance can throw off your vocal technique. Your balance begins with making sure your voice is well supported with air—in other words, taking a deep enough breath and then regulating the air flow with your diaphragm muscle. Next, your larynx and vocal cords need to be relaxed and able to vibrate freely. Once the air passes your vocal cords and becomes sound, it is then manipulated using your articulators. Speaking on balance and on breath gives the perception that the sound, the words, and the ideas are flowing out of you. This can often be described as your voice having a lyrical quality with forward momentum. Now that you know what the goal is, let's look at some common speech behaviors that can steal the air that you need for effective speech.

The shaky start. The first point at which many individuals leak air is before they even make a sound! Make sure you don't give away all of your vocal fuel, your means of relaxation, your comfort, and your confidence by exhaling through your nose and then speaking. You may be one of the individuals who has convince themselves that you don't actually breathe when you speak, or perhaps you never really thought about it. Either way you have to recognize how important it is to harness and control the use of your breath. Don't allow air to leak through your nose before you even have a chance to use it for speech.

Exercises for recognizing breath support. The following exercise is fine for recognizing the sensation of breath support. Additional exercises in this chapter will help you refine and adjust the use of breath for speaking longer phrases and sentences. It is essential that you know what speaking "on breath" feels like.

First, inhale slowly for about two to three seconds; hold your breath. Be conscious of not allowing any breath to escape through your nose. Speak each of these short phrases separately, taking a fresh breath at the start of each one.

Give them an inch.
Now I understand.
Do we have a plan?

Better safe than sorry.
What comes next?
That's what I mean.
Vote with your head.

You will probably hear that your voice is noticeably louder when well supported. It may even sound as if you're shouting the words. Harnessing your breath is the only way to eventually be able to physically relax your voice enough to change your delivery from shouting to assertive and confident speech.

Bursting onto the scene. Pushing too much air at the very start of speaking is a speech behavior known as bursting. You can recognize this behavior in speakers whose sentences start strong but constantly trail off due to their running out of air. You may recognize yourself becoming stuck in the behavioral cycle of releasing all of your air right in the beginning of a sentence. This leaves very little breath to use when trying to finish in a definitive matter.

Exercises for regulating airflow. The balance needed to start strong and end strong requires regulating your airflow using your diaphragm muscle. Knowing that there is important information near the end of a sentence will help you learn how to hold onto a bit of your vocal fuel.

Speak the following sentences as if in slow motion. Pause at the comma after the phrases without taking a second breath.

In retrospect, the research took longer than expected.
Knowing your risk tolerance, we should look elsewhere.
If there are no further questions, let's end the call for today.
In the span of three years, we have seen tremendous growth.
After a long day, you just want to relax.
Before you go, please get me the updated numbers.

Running out of air as you speak will cause the pace of your speech to increase. Try those sentences again and slow down an additional 20 percent. It may feel agonizingly slow, but this is the only way to adjust your vocal balance point.

Don't let me down. We have already discussed the possibility of air leaking through your nose before you start to speak. Air can also leak through your nose at the end of a sentence. This sudden release of air indicates a relaxing or releasing of your diaphragm muscle. You don't want to draw attention to your exhalation, as this repetitive speech behavior can be mistaken for tiredness or exasperation. It can also lead to a feeling of giving up on the end of your sentences. Believe it or not, the time to relax is while you are speaking, not in between your sentences or phrases. Efficient diaphragm regulation will lead to an increased feeling of relaxation and comfort. Remember you don't need to release all of the air in your lungs before taking another deep, deliberate breath.

Exercises for controlled sentence endings. Take a deliberate breath and then try speaking the first sentence below, pausing without taking an additional breath at the ellipsis after the words *about* and *the*. Hold onto any remaining breath after speaking the last word of the sentence for two seconds, then deliberately release the air from your lungs. Take another deliberate breath and follow the same pattern for all of the sentences.

I know a thing or two about . . . the . . . subject.
Let me give you an overview of last . . . week's . . . numbers.
Have you thought . . . about . . . the project anymore?
Stop trying to put words . . . in . . . my mouth.
We need our brand to resonate . . . with a wider . . . demographic.
Ladies and Gentlemen of the jury . . . consider . . . all . . . of the facts.

Being able to stop and start efficiently shows an enormous amount of speech control. It sends the message that you are in charge of what comes next. You are the one driving the bus. Remember that the silence in between is as important as the words you say.

The importance of being voiceless. A lot of air leaks when you're speaking your voiceless consonant sounds, if you don't know what they are. So, what is the difference between a voiceless and a voiced consonant sound? A voiced consonant sound uses or engages your vocal cords, whereas a voiceless sound does not. This makes an enormous difference in the sounds you speak. Here are the voiceless and voiced consonant sounds frequently used in American English. Notice that the voiced consonants below each voiceless consonant use the exact same articulation, except that vocal cord vibration is added.

Voiceless Consonants: *p, t, f, k, s, sh, ch, th*
Voiced Consonants: *B, D, V, G, Z, ZH, DJ, TH*

There is a direct relationship between recognizing voiceless consonant sounds and compensating for overarticulation. Never try to make a voiceless consonant sound as loud as a voiced consonant. They are simply two very different types of acoustic sounds. Attempting to do this will cause you to leak a lot of air. Not only does it throw off your vocal balance but also pushing too much air through a voiceless sound can cause your voice to become breathy or puffy sounding. No one likes to sound "soft" in business.

Exercises for voiceless consonant recognition. The voiceless consonant sounds in the following sentences are all underlined. Be aware that these are the sounds in which it is easiest to leak air. You need to soften your articulation or pull back the amount of air you push through the underlined sounds.

Placing someone in a forward facing position should be in keeping with a company's culture.

People fail to factor time into their plan for financial success.

Clients insist that changes should be forthcoming. (The *T* at the end of *that* is a glottal T.)

If you forward me the statement, I can quickly show the chairman the offense. (The *T* at the end of *statement* is a glottal T.)

First, we need to search the current field of applicants for a good fit. (There are glottal Ts at the end of *current, applicant,* and *fit.*)

We should all search for something more suited to the purpose. (The *T* in *suited* is pronounced as a soft *D*, and the *D* is a glottal D.)

At first, it may seem as if you're just speaking softer. Soon you will get used to pushing air through large vowel sounds and not through the voiceless consonant sounds. Your vocal balance will shift slightly and your overall volume will increase.

Got glottal? Two of the most important continuity devices at your disposal are the glottal T and the glottal D. A glottal stop is a type of consonant sound produced by obstructing airflow in the vocal tract or, more precisely, the glottis. Many languages use glottal sounds. In American English, the airflow is stopped by synchronizing a holding of the diaphragm muscle and the touching of the tip of the tongue to the roof of your mouth just above the gum ridge. This stop of airflow indicates that the T or D is being spoken. The glottal articulations allow you to speak difficult combinations of voiceless or voiced consonant sounds smoothly. The lack of ability to execute this articulation can also be a major source of air leakage.

Exercises for integrating glottal Ts and Ds. Try speaking each of the sentences below. Then go over each notated word to recognize the complex integration of glottal sounds. Some of the written Ts will change from a voiceless T to voiced D and vice versa. Luckily, you will probably know how to articulate the majority of these sounds correctly.

That lawsuit demonstrates the importance of settling matters in writing.
That: glottal T on the end
lawsuit: glottal T on the end
demonstrates: the second T is glottal
importance: glottal T
settling: the double T is a glottal D because of the following L articulation
matters: the double T is a soft D
writing: the T becomes a soft D

The merits of the hedge fund were judged to be completely fabricated.
merits: glottal T
hedge: glottal D
judged: the first D is a glottal D
completely: glottal T
fabricated: the T becomes a soft D

For the record, I am not impressed with your dramatic threats.
record: glottal D
impressed: the D becomes a voiceless T because it is followed by voiceless S
dramatic: the T becomes a soft D
threats: glottal T

Expert advice would have significantly increased the client's insight.
Expert: glottal T
advice: glottal D
would: glottal D
significantly: glottal T
increased: the D normally becomes a voiceless T, here it becomes a glottal T
client's: glottal T
insight: glottal T

Critical improvements were overlooked in the updated budget.
Critical: the T becomes a soft D

improvements: glottal T
overlooked: the D becomes a voiceless T
updated: the T becomes a soft D
budget: glottal D and glottal T

Did she demonstrate the same pattern of evaluating without listening?
Did: glottal D
demonstrate: glottal T
pattern: the double T becomes a soft D
evaluating: the T becomes a soft D
without: glottal T on the end
listening: glottal T

Being aware that glottal sounds are the right articulation to use can be very empowering. It is important to always actively use your tongue and diaphragm together to reduce tension surrounding your glottis. Use them correctly, often, and in a relaxed manner.

Face the facts. Articulating too hard can have an effect on your outward appearance too. There is the potential for unwanted perceptions to be projected to anyone listening or watching. You can fall into the habit of overworking your lips if you try to make your voiceless P and your voiced B sounds too plosive. Many individuals exaggerate their lip articulation on their nasal Ms. Overarticulating voiceless T and F can cause your mouth to spread too wide. Pushing voiceless SH and CH can make you push your lips too far forward. Overarticulating W can push your lips forward too. Your upper lip may actually rise on one side or the other if you are consistently pushing too much air through your voiceless S sound. Struggling with articulation is often mistaken for struggling with words, ideas, or even emotions. Consistent overarticulation can give you the sensation of tightness in your cheeks and especially in your jaw.

Exercises for unnecessary facial movements. Speak the following sentences while looking in the mirror. Watch for any exaggerated lip movements.

Manage potential whenever possible.
Let's focus on patterns in the broader markets.
We don't typically choose to work faster.

The boycott matters to the people in charge.
Changing bank regulations could possibly affect future returns.
Should you tell a team member when they have missed something?

The reduction in unnecessary lip movement may create an urge to express too much with your eyebrows. As an alternative to tightening your articulation or using your eyebrows, try gesturing more fully. A very simple outstretching of the hands as you deliver your words should suffice for this exercise.

Catch Some ZZZs. One of the fastest ways to self-correct leaking too much air on voiceless consonants is to focus on the voiced Z sound. You may be hard-pressed to come up with more than two-dozen commonly used words that actually have the letter Z in them. Yet we use the voiced Z sound constantly. It is almost always disguised as the letter S. You will discover the voiced Z sound whenever the plural S is added to words that end in a voiced consonant sound, such as *labs*, *kids*, *lives*, *dogs*, *roses*, *wages*, and *clothes*. The voiced Z is used when the plural S is added to words that end in R, such as *cars* or *fingers*. Adding the plural S to nasal sounds also creates a voiced Z articulation, as in *plans*, *firms*, and *things*, or when *es* is added as in *branches* or *sizes*. Many small words that you use constantly also contain the voiced Z disguised as S: *is*, *was*, *as*, and *has*.

Exercises for Z and S sounds. The voiced Zs disguised as Ss are underlined in the following sentences. Focus on articulating the voiced Zs very deliberately. Don't worry about overarticulating your voiced Zs in this exercise. You need to become more aware of the sensation of engaging your vocal cords when making this sound.

Substantial investor enthusiasm caused the banks to adjust their positions.
    Team members expressed doubts about raising the prices.
    His managers advised him to make no mistakes on the proposal.
    Office policy describes all of the necessary rules and expectations.
    The notes from the meetings were more guidelines than instructions.
    Interviewers have a system of questions that expose less desirable candidates.

At first, correcting your articulation of voiced Z will feel very odd indeed. Trust that using your vocal cords in this manner will allow less air to leak out. For most people, voiceless S is the leakiest consonant sound. The voiced Zs are the key!

This and that. Recognizing the difference between voiceless TH and voiced TH can be even trickier than voiceless S and voiced Z. The position in precision of placing your tongue is the key to making the difference. Your tongue should be just behind your upper teeth when articulating a voiceless TH in words such as *with* or *both*. If you allow your tongue to touch your teeth while making this sound, it will sound like a voiceless T, and *with* becomes *wit* and *both* become *boat*. When articulating your voiced TH sound, your tongue needs to almost touch the edge of your upper teeth, allowing your tongue to vibrate with your vocal cords in words such as *mother* and *that*. Pushing your tongue too hard against your teeth will change the sound into a voiced D, and *mother* becomes *mudder* and *that* becomes *dat*.

Exercises for recognizing TH sounds. Now that you know there is a very clear difference between voiceless and voiced TH, try speaking the sentences below. The voiced TH sounds are underlined, and the voiceless TH sounds are marked by a line above. Remember voiceless TH is a lighter, softer sound. Be careful to not let too much air escape with voiceless TH.

Neither knew whether both third- and fourth-quarter profits would strengthen.
They thought a thorough investigation from within would further their cause.
Nothing but authentic enthusiasm could sustain that monthly growth.
Those theorists will argue almost anything without thinking for themselves.
The otherwise truthful therapist would rather say nothing than threaten his career.
Thousands of healthcare professionals could not weather the lengthy, in-depth training.

TH sounds give many of my clients the most trouble. Not being aware that there are two different TH sounds can really leave you feeling tongue-tied. Remember that voiced TH uses your vocal cords and vibrates and voiceless TH is light and airy—but not too airy! You want to keep the leakage to a minimum while still articulating correctly and smoothly.

10

More Than Words
Body Language Techniques

Gesturing refers to hand and body movements that support a spoken or unspoken message. Supportive gestures come from following your impulses when speaking. They are always there. You just need to become accustomed to the practice of tapping into them consistently. Luckily, breathing is at the center of learning how to discover your gestures. Varying your gestures is as important as finding them. There is an enormous amount of creativity that goes into exploring the possibilities. The sense of spontaneity will hold your listeners' attention and make your message more compelling. You will be giving off the perception of being "in the moment." Holding one gesture until the impulse for the next gesture comes along allows for unspoken continuity in your storytelling.

Clearing the way. Gesturing eases the flow of spoken words, phrases, and sentences. It has a direct effect on the rhythm of your speech. Gestures can be used to punctuate, emphasize, support, and add nuance to everything you say. They also give you, the speaker, a stronger sense of commitment and connection to the words you're saying. Surprisingly, many people don't know the first thing about gesturing and are actually uncomfortable when trying to do it. Wrapping your head around the fact that there are an unlimited number of gestures may not help. It is important to start with a small number of gestures that work consistently, and then build from there.

Exercises for adding gestures. Let's begin with seven common and effective gestures that you should become more comfortable using. I have given them names for quick reference and recognition. Try each of them out slowly at first. You can then begin slightly increasing the pace of your delivery.

1. The Rewind: pointed finger drawing a small circle (try with each hand individually)
2. The Either Or: palms facing upward alternating raising and falling
3. The Ball of Wax: hands surrounding a small ball
4. The Hammer: a clenched fist softly hitting the open palm of your other hand (try alternating hands)
5. The Back There: a closed hand with your thumb extended pointing behind you (try with each hand individually)
6. The No Way: palms facing downward, one over the other at the start and motioning away from each other to opposite sides
7. The Authentic: palm open moving toward and lightly touching your chest

Once you are comfortable executing these seven gestures, use the following short phrases to practice speaking and gesturing together:

1. "If we back ahead," "before we do that," "Let's go back"
2. "either, or," "people are undecided," "yes and no"
3. "bring it together," "what we have here," "let's start with a concept"
4. "we need to work hard," "this has to stop," "find the strength to change"
5. "last year," "we know all of this," "put it behind us"
6. "never again," "not on my watch," "there is no other way"
7. "I have learned so much," "but we can do more," "this means a lot to me"

Push through the initial observation that it feels forced. It's like giving up at the gym after one day. Don't do it! There are enormous benefits to be gained. You will feel more comfortable the more you practice the gestures as described.

Fresh cooking. Now that you have a few new gestures to play with, don't fall in love with them and use them to death. Even the most interesting and connected gestures can become boring when repeated too often.

Creative gesturing is an ongoing process. Hopefully, trying out some new gestures has started to unlock your gesturing potential. Always follow your impulses. This will lead you to finding creative and supportive gestures.

Following your impulses means following the feeling in your body, in your gut. It is the same feeling you have when speaking in a casual setting with friends and family. You probably don't even think about following impulses, but they are still at work.

Exercises for creative gesturing. Referencing the initial gestures above, let's look at some alternate gestures that can be used when speaking the same short phrases. Notice how each gesture alters the meaning and the intonation; that is, the rhythm and pitch, of a phrase. These are the subtle nuances you are looking to project.

1. The Here and Now: open hand starting near the chest and dropping slowly to waist height (try with each hand individually)
2. The This or That: both hands, parallel to each other and a few inches apart, landing on one side of your body and then the opposite side
3. The Big Picture: palms at chest height, facing down, one over the other at the start, that move downward at the same rate, outlining a globe shape
4. The Hard Work: hands clenched at chest, as if holding ski poles, and motioning downward together
5. The Mover: both on your right side, right hand open toward the body and left hand out, move simultaneously to your left side switching in and out positions (try starting on the left and moving to the right.)
6. The Wait a Minute: open palms out, at chest height, pull back slightly and then move forward with an abrupt stop
7. The Heartfelt: one open palm on chest while the other open hand starts at the chest and slowly moves down to waist height

You are now beginning the process of expanding your repertoire and increasing your comfort level. Try using the notes of an upcoming presentation, or the minutes from a prior meeting, to look for opportunities to integrate some of these gesturing ideas. You cannot gesture too often when practicing this extended exercise.

Gesturing ETA. Where you land your gestures while speaking will determine their effectiveness. You should start the delivery of your gesture slightly ahead of the word you want to emphasize. This approach will aid in the sense of flow. Deliberate anticipation will keep your gestures from seeming rushed or as if they're coming out of nowhere. They will support the words you are speaking in a very definitive way.

Exercises for timing your gestures. Speak the following group of sentences out loud. Be conscious of maintaining a steady, even pace when speaking.

We find ourselves at a crossroads between growing the company and maintaining brand integrity. Overall, things look optimistic. But, have we taken the time to determine where we're going? We have to ask ourselves, "What really matters?"

Now add the specific gesture that corresponds with each phrase. Make sure you land the designated gesture on the underlined word in the phrase. Remember to anticipate the landing of each gesture. Try each gesture and phrase combination separately before trying to put them together in complete sentences.

The Here and Now: We <u>find</u> ourselves at a crossroads
The This or That: between <u>growing</u> the company and <u>maintaining</u> brand integrity.
The Big Picture: <u>Overall</u>, things look optimistic.
The Hard Work: But, have we <u>taken</u> the time
The Mover: to determine <u>where</u> we're going?
The Wait a Minute: We <u>have</u> to ask ourselves,
The Heartfelt: "What <u>really</u> matters?"

Notice that gestures don't have to follow a pattern of always falling on the verb in a sentence, and they certainly don't always fall on the first word. In fact, you have the flexibility to change where you land your gestures. Try the same exercise with different underlined words receiving the gesture.

The Here and Now: <u>We</u> find ourselves at a crossroads
The This or That: between growing the <u>company</u> and maintaining brand <u>integrity</u>.

The Big Picture: Overall, things <u>look</u> optimistic.
The Hard Work: But, <u>have</u> we taken the time
The Mover: to <u>determine</u> where we're going?
The Wait a Minute: We have to <u>ask</u> ourselves
The Heartfelt: "What really <u>matters</u>?"

This integration of gestures will quite noticeably slow down your pace. They are meant to do that. Gestures project a higher level of commitment to the words you're speaking. They also give you a feeling of being more grounded in your delivery.

No bouncing please! Don't fall into the trap of overemphasizing your gestures in an effort to really get your point across. In other words, don't bounce those gestures! Deliver each gesture once and with confidence; hold it in place, as if you are allowing your listeners to fully comprehend the meaning of your words and your body language. This simple adjustment to your gesturing will project an amazing amount of confidence.

Exercises for holding gestures. Use the sentences and corresponding gestures from above to recognize and ultimately regulate gesturing continuity. Continuity is the smooth transition between both your spoken words and between your gestures. Once you land the gesture, hold it until it is time for the next one. Push through the initial awkwardness of holding your gestures as you practice.

We (Here and Now) <u>find</u> ourselves at a crossroads between (This or . . .) <u>growing</u> the company and (. . . or That) <u>maintaining</u> brand integrity. (Big Picture) <u>Overall</u>, things look optimistic. But, (Hard Work) <u>have</u> we taken the time to (Mover) <u>determine</u> where we're going? We have to (Wait a Minute) <u>ask</u> ourselves, "What (Heartfelt) <u>really</u> matters?"

Try reading a passage from a novel or from the newspaper, and follow your impulses that will lead you to appropriate and supportive gesturing. Maintain the discipline of holding each gesture until the impulse for the next gesture comes along.

Own the silence. Many speakers consider the silence between spoken words to be "awkward pauses" or "awkward silence." For many this can be one of the greatest challenges to confident speech. Some mistakenly try to cover the silence by speaking faster and in continuous run-on sentences. This kind of challenge is also an opportunity. The individual who can own the silence can easily own the room, or at least exude an enormous amount of confidence.

There are three parts to owning the silence. First, you need to breathe deeply; then you have to hold your gesture in mid-delivery, along with looking away slightly as if deep in thought. Don't try to hide that you are collecting your ideas and determining what you're going to say next. Listeners are intrigued by your thought process. It is the unguarded moment that they actually want to see—but probably don't realize it. Deliver the gesture first and then speak the words. Your comfort in owning the silence speaks volumes in regard to your confidence.

Exercises for gesturing between words. For this advanced exercise, use the seven initial gestures offered earlier in this chapter. Review what they are and how to execute them. Elongate the anticipation of landing your gesture. In baseball terms, it is the long wind-up. Once again, make sure you hold the gesture until the very end of the sentence. Don't let go too soon. Take a deliberate breath; hold it as you begin your gesture; then say the corresponding sentence.

The Rewind: "Let's go back to a point you brought up earlier."
The Either Or: "I'm on the fence about that."
The Ball of Wax: "All of the due diligence has been done."
The Hammer: "We have to find a way to get this done."
The Back There: "That was good enough yesterday."
The No Way: "Look, there has got to be a better way."
The Authentic: "I was surprised when I heard the news."

Once you are able to execute the timing of these gestures smoothly, try all seven in a row. Make sure you breathe before each one. Your hands and your body should always appear active and engaged.

I caught a fish THIS big. I often hear the concern that gesturing might seem over the top or too big. No matter how big or intimate the setting is, your gestures should be full. What I mean by full is grounded in your body in a way that makes you feel connected—in other words, speech as a full-body experience. Your gestures should make you feel as if you are "in the moment," and they should project the same sense of confidence and commitment. Of course, gesturing always needs to be adjusted to scale. You can base these adjustments on the number of listeners, the size of venue, or the type of media with which you're being viewed or listened to. Don't forget that gesturing is an important part of nonvisual communication too. Abandoning full gestures when your listeners can't see you is running the risk of sounding disconnected and potentially losing your forward momentum.

Exercises for adjusting to scale. Use all of the gestures suggested and described in this chapter to experience the similarities between large and small gesturing. Remember the gesture is the same. The size and amount of space increases or decreases based on the communication scenario.

The first sentence of each pair of sentences is meant to be delivered to a very large crowd. Don't be afraid to really go for it. Make sure you don't fling your gestures or just stab at them in an attempt to make them seem large. They need to be delivered with confidence and held until you have completed your statement.

The second sentence of each pair should be delivered as if you are sitting close to a single listener. Even though the scale is much smaller, you still need to be fully committed to your gesturing. Avoid the temptation to pull back on a gesture simply because the scale is so small. Hold on to it for maximum effectiveness.

The Rewind (Big): "Take a moment to look around the room."
The Rewind (Small): "Explain to me again where the money will come from."

The Either Or (Big): "Both options have merit."
The Either Or (Small): "It's a little unclear where you stand on this issue."

The Ball of Wax (Big): "We have an opportunity here to make a change."
The Ball of Wax (Small): "I need you to understand how important this is to me."

The Hammer (Big): "Do what is right."
The Hammer (Small): "That's why we can't wait any longer."

The Back There (Big): "We cannot ignore our responsibilities."
The Back There (Small): "That was a long time ago."

The No Way (Big): "No one has all the facts in this case."
The No Way (Small): "I can't be associated with that."

The Authentic (Big): "Thank you so much for this tremendous honor."
The Authentic (Small): "That was a very special time in my life."

The Here and Now (Big): "Let's begin the meeting with a quick update."
The Here and Now (Small): "I'd like to hear what you think."

The This or That (Big): "The teachers and the administrators have to work together."
The This or That (Small): "Should we follow tradition or try something new?"

The Big Picture (Big): "It can all come together in time."
The Big Picture (Small): "Perhaps we can smooth over our apparent differences."

The Hard Work (Big): "We can't allow ourselves to be distracted."
The Hard Work (Small): "I need you to support me on this issue."

The Mover (Big): "Do we just expect things to change overnight?"
The Mover (Small): "Yes, the project is almost completed."

The Wait a Minute (Big): "I know what you're thinking."
The Wait a Minute (Small): "Please listen to the whole story."

The Heartfelt (Big): "I've said these things over and over."
The Heartfelt (Small): "I will gladly consider what you're asking."

Gesturing is an essential part of conveying any message. Your gestures may not always be smooth, but your transitions and your commitment should be clear. This is the level of comfort and confidence you are looking to feel and project. Your listeners will also be comfortable knowing that you're the one driving the bus and you are taking them on the journey.

Follow the face. Facial expressions are an important part of your overall body language. Opening your mouth when creating more vowel space will certainly free your face to be more animated. However, undesirable facial movements are usually the result of overarticulation. Tension in your articulators and your mouth can lead to repetitive expressions that most speakers are unaware of. A constant smile and habitual lip movements can be distracting and can give off the unintended perceptions of being disingenuous or being nervous. Eyebrows that are too expressive can be attributed to a lack of supportive gesturing. Facial expressions should be allowed to develop free of any articulation or gesturing issues.

Ready, willing, and able. Facial expressions, in general, should project the level of interest that you want you listeners to have. Effective interactions occur when both parties show that they are ready, willing, and able to share their perspectives. Your face should reflect your willingness to engage.

Exercises for preparing to speak. The tip of your tongue should touch your hard palate very lightly in the same position as when you're articulating a D, an N, or a T. This will add brightness to your face as you anticipate speaking. First, find the D, N, and T tongue position by making each sound three times and then moving on to the next sound. Then, hold your tongue in that position with your lips closed as you take a breath.

Taking a deliberate inhalation of breath when you are about to speak will cause your head to rise slightly and your face to "brighten." This body language sends the message that you are ready to take charge. It can also signal that you have an inquisitive nature, or perhaps that your interest has been piqued by what someone else has said.

Slave to articulation. There are active and passive articulators involved in making consonant sounds. Active articulators are the ones that can be manipulated or touched within your mouth. In very basic terms, you use your tongue, your teeth, your lips, your hard palate (the roof of your mouth), and your soft palate. These organs can be further divided into sections— the tip of your tongue, or the gum ridge, which is a specific part of your hard palate. Although articulation takes place in your mouth, it can actually show up on your face. Visibly overactive lips and eyebrows and incorrect mouth positions can all result from articulating too hard.

You may experience only one or two of these conditions consistently or only from time to time. Circumstances may cause the condition to flare up, especially when nerves start to get the better of you. Shallow breathing always leads to more tense articulation. Couple this with an overall feeling of being tight when you're put on the spot and you have a recipe for very nervous, repetitive speech behavior.

Exercises for recognizing facial issues. No one will ever tell you that you are making seemingly odd expressions and facial movements, but they will notice it. You need to overcome your reluctance to watch yourself speak in order to discover if you're guilty of this behavior. Using your laptop or phone, record yourself speaking the following paragraph. Make sure you speak these words with energy and passion, using good breath support and forward momentum:

Steve, I don't know why you and your team didn't hear me the first time! Please move the Tuesday meeting to Friday. We need more time to strengthen our case! I don't feel the opening statement has enough punch. Do you have any idea when these strategic matters can be reviewed? People close to the case believe we are foolish for not seeing this sooner. Can you please call me back ASAP?!

There are several telltale signs that you are overarticulating and working harder than you have to. Focus on your eyebrows, your lips, and the movements of your mouth. Determine for yourself if any of your speech behaviors could be an unnecessary distraction to the true meaning of your message.

Wipe that smile. Speaking with a constant smile is a speech condition known as *spread*. It stems from having too much tension in your jaw and articulators. Because the jaw can't relax and open freely, your mouth starts to open horizontally. This condition develops slowly over time. Most people who suffer from spread are usually not aware that they are doing it. Many complain that, at times, their cheeks hurt, but they don't know why. The cure is to think vertically.

Exercises for reducing spread with vowels. The long *ee* vowel sound is the usual trigger that leads to spread. It is also a part of other long vowel sounds: long *i* and long *ae*. Speak each combination of words below five times in a row. Increase the relaxation of the sides of your mouth and your cheeks each time. There is no need to record yourself speaking the word combinations. Reducing spread requires knowing the sensation of staying vertical. Allow the vowels to resonate freely inside your mouth.

easy breezy
high time
play the game
meet me
by nine
many days
see the eagle
straight line
sustain gains
my ear
safe place
east of here

You will probably feel a little "stone-faced" at first. Stay disciplined. You need to have a very deliberate approach to getting your face to truly relax.

Elvis lips. Any Elvis Presley impersonator will tell you that you can't really do Elvis without his signature lip twitch. It was part of his persona—part of his charisma. But it did nothing at all for his articulation. There are several unnecessary lip movements that are all caused by overarticulation of consonant sounds or the improper placement of vowel sounds. The most notable culprits are: voiced B, nasal M, and voiceless SH, the combination of STR, and the vowel sounds long *ee* and long *oo*. We have already talked about the long *ee* vowel sound causing the mouth to spread. Protruding lips can also creep into the making of the R sound. Some individuals add lip tension to the making of this sound, which can almost look as if they are baring their teeth.

Be mindful of pushing too much air on voiceless S, voiceless F, and voiceless P. The extra push of air has to go somewhere! It will usually cause either one side of your upper lip to rise or one side of your lower lip to fall slightly.

Exercises for reducing lip movement. Try speaking the following sentences while being aware of keeping your lips as relaxed as possible. Video recording yourself is the fastest way to determine if you are sabotaging your speech technique with unnecessary lip movements.

Take special note of any sounds that make you feel as if you're leaking air. Certainly any sounds that whistle are a red flag that you're pushing too much air and your articulation needs to be adjusted.

Dancing eyebrows. Unnecessary eyebrow movements are another repetitive speech behavior. Overactive eyebrows, or dancing eyebrows, are not a direct result of overarticulation. There is a very strong link between too much eyebrow movement and too little supportive gesturing. If you don't ground your energy in your body with gestures, it will find its way onto your face, especially in your eyebrows. The energy of communication has to go somewhere!

Exercises for facial relaxation. Even the slightest gesture, as long as it's full, will reduce the urge to express too much with your eyebrows. This is not to say that you should not use your eyebrows in an appropriate way. You don't want your face to be expressionless.

Use the group of sentences again, but this time add very deliberate gestures to your delivery. You should feel your face relax as you feel more connected to your body. This is speech as a full-body exercise.

Fool me once (gesture the number one), shame on you (point ahead); fool me twice (gesture the number two), shame on me (gesture back to your chest).

The sooner we leave (both hands sweeping in front of your torso), the better chance we have of staying on schedule (pointing on the words *staying*, *on*, and *schedule*).

Meet me on Tuesday (point down) and we'll instruct the team on recent developments (parallel hands turning in a synchronized clockwise motion).

You should feel fine (palms down, pushing out from in front of your waist to either side) by the time you finally arrive today (palms flipped up).

The structure of the deal (two parallel fists moving downward from shoulder height and stopping at the waist) was such that I couldn't say "no" (palms flipped upward).

I (fingertips to chest) believe that people have strong feelings about how (one hand pointing) to spend their Saturdays.

Tap into your ability to use gestures fully. Make sure you are not stopping yourself short or holding back the flow from gesture to gesture. Relaxing your face will increase your sense of comfort when speaking. It will also project a persona of confidence to your listeners.

The 80/50 Rule. Getting your point across means connecting with your listeners. This connection is initiated through good eye contact. There is a tender balance between too much and too little. The majority of your eye contact, and therefore your attention, is actually given while you are listening—not while you're speaking. Trying to change this balance due to your desire to really connect can lead to unwanted results. As you might imagine, the balance of eye contact changes based on the number of people you're speaking with and whether you are in a conversation, in a meeting, or addressing a large group. There are some general rules about what it is appropriate, what is creepy, and what is truly powerful.

The right imbalance. A good conversation is a balance of speaking and listening. It is also a balance of eye contact. I refer to that balance as the 80/50 Rule. It describes the percentage of time you should be making direct eye contact when listening and when speaking. As a listener you are generally making direct eye contact with the speaker 80 percent of the time. However, when you're speaking, you look at your listener only about 50 percent of the time. Obviously, the percentages keep shifting as each individual changes roles in the conversation. The lesser percentage when speaking means that you are looking away more often as you continue from one thought to the next. This allows your listener an unguarded moment to look into your thought process. The gap in eye contact will still hold their focus and actually help to draw them deeper into understanding the importance of your words.

The look away. As important as good eye contact is, there is also a need to look away from time to time, usually when you are collecting your thoughts. It should be done in a clear and definitive way. You have a right to do it, and you should do it without apology. The body language of looking away sends a message that you are truly present and in the moment. If you do it with confidence, it looks as if you are truly considering what you are about to say. This can be hard to do when it is your turn to speak at a meeting. You feel as if all eyes are on you and there is nowhere to hide. Confident speakers can signal the importance of their message and still hold their listeners' focus by looking away.

Spot on. How you look away and where you look away are important details to consider and perfect. It is important to remember to never look too far off center when speaking to an individual, a small group, or a crowd. You never want to make it seem as if you've suddenly noticed something stuck to the ceiling, crawling on the floor, or sneaking up on either side of you. That would be extremely distracting. Pick a spot that is just slightly different from where you would gaze as you're speaking. Remember that this rule is magnified whenever you find yourself on camera.

The Death Stare. There is a dark side to eye contact too. The fear of losing a listener's attention can lead to too much eye contact. A speaker who locks eyes and won't let go is guilty of the Death Stare. The intentions are good but the results are not. When a listener becomes aware of too much eye contact coming from a speaker, they feel as if they are the ones being put on the spot. They can't look away for fear of disrespecting the speaker. This can make the connection a little too intense, a little uncomfortable, and a little creepy. If you find that your conversations have a tendency to end quickly and you don't know why, consider that your eye contact may be too intense for your listener. Project the confidence that comes with knowing that you already have their attention.

Field of vision. When speaking to a small group, make sure you make eye contact with each individual during any extended speaking. Don't let your eyes and head snap to the next person; simply allow your gaze to find them. Try using the space between individuals as your spot for looking away. Don't always follow the same pattern of left to right or right to left. Your eye contact should not become a predictable part of your body language.

When addressing a large group, don't just look over the tops of people's heads. Your listeners can tell that you're doing it, and it looks as if you are reticent to engage. You have their attention; they are looking at you. Look back with the same eagerness and authenticity as you "take it all in."

Video conferencing savvy. When you are teleconferencing with a group in the room, you always need to be aware of where the camera is. Consider including moments where you look directly into the camera for added connection. Treat the camera like one of the individuals who is physically in the room.

It is important to remember that even the smallest movements will be magnified by the camera. Your "looking away spot" should only be an inch or two from the camera lens. Avoid looking anywhere above the camera lens. This behavior is extremely distracting to anyone watching. Always choose to look slightly below the camera in those moments that call for looking away; for example, as you're gathering your thoughts, remembering some details, or considering some information for the first time.

Eye contact does not have to be continuous to be effective. Being aware of the general rules and the need for adjustments will help you recognize when your balance may be a little off. Your initial connection with your listener(s) will almost always start with direct eye contact, but you can really draw them in by knowing how and when to look away for effect.

11

Of Tall Tales and Bumper Stickers
Preparation Tricks

A bumper sticker is the shortest way of describing what you want to say and why you want to say it. It presumes that you have already filtered all of the important information and details through your perspective and have come up with a descriptive phrase, short enough to fit on a car bumper sticker. Because it is an expression that includes both your perspective and your understanding, your bumper sticker will help you stay on track and immediately establish a framework that makes it easier for your listeners to follow you. Learning to find your bumper sticker in the overwhelming amount of information and possibilities about your topic is a very worthwhile discipline. It is the key to staying focused on your agenda and to delivering a compelling narrative.

VIP POV! Bumper stickers are bold, and they are powerful. They always carry your opinion, even if your objective is to be objective. What you choose to include and exclude in any presentation or conversation is based on your perspective—what *you* believe is important. Trying to leave your point of view out of it is a recipe for failure. A strong storyteller always delivers a clear perspective. It is an essential element to being both interesting and compelling. By being bold, you are offering an intriguing point of view that demands further explanation. Your explanation consists of the three main reasons you feel the way you do about the subject. I use the word *feel* very deliberately because the process of finding a bumper sticker is more visceral than intellectual. Once again authenticity must trump intelligence. It begins with believing how important your perspective is. It begins with believing in your bumper stickers.

Lowering the light show. There are always a lot of things that you can convince yourself need to be considered in any business communication scenario. Such as:

> the need to be right,
> the need to make good impressions,
> the need to be comfortable,
> the need to connect,
> the need to overcome your fears,
> the need to cover it all,
> and the need to be prepared for the unexpected.

It can be easy to get lost in the light show of possibilities and information. You have to get past the need to show everyone how smart you are and simply let it be a given. Your job is to deliver a clear story with a sense of forward momentum. Your story needs to sound as if it's "going somewhere."

This is not to say that you should abandon the required due diligence in knowing your subject. Once you have a strong grasp on the topic at hand, you have to adjust your approach when it comes to delivering your message. Your focus should be on the experience, not on the information. This is called adopting the four-thousand-foot view. You only need the important facts that support the telling of the experiential side of the story. Remind yourself that your listeners can always ask for further details. Leaving them wanting more creates a desirable level of engagement.

Trimming the fat. Overstuffing a presentation or a conversation is a common speaking mistake. You increase the clarity and power of your message by learning how to distill information. Streamlining your presentation is always a plus in your fast-paced business world. It is also crucial to the process of discovering your bumper stickers. Write down the three factual reasons for believing what you believe to be true about your topic. I know it sounds very reminiscent of the standard format for a college essay, but simple works! If you find that you have more than three concepts, discipline yourself to combine ideas; you can always separate them later upon request. Speak about them out loud until you realize the single characterization of all three. It should always be as short a phrase as possible.

I realize that it flies in the face of the urge to overstuff and jump right into massive amounts of detail. Brevity of message brings clarity. Once you think it's short enough, try making your bumper sticker even shorter. This approach anchors you as a speaker, gives your listeners room to process, and offers you the flexibility to include new information and perspectives from other participating individuals.

Buried treasure. The concept of bumper stickers sounds wonderful in theory, but putting it into practice can be a little tricky. You find your bumper sticker by recognizing the three reasons that brought you to discovering it. But the three reasons have to come from the bumper sticker. So, which comes first, the chicken or the egg? Start by asking yourself, "Why am I delivering this message?" Your initial response may be because your boss told you to or because you really want to make some good impressions. In other words, it feels like an obligation. Dig a little deeper. Get to the mindset where you are thinking about what interests you about your message and why it is important to communicate it. Now imagine someone asking you the following question in a very dismissive way: "Why does *that* matter?" Allow your quick, silent response to be, "It matters because . . . " You may be surprised by what your knee-jerk reaction is. Next, repeat the same dismissive question but speak your response out loud. Always let your gesturing and body language come along for the ride. You will be tapping into a wealth of authenticity that is undeniable.

Bumper sticker example. This book is chock-full of bumper stickers. There is certainly an enormous amount of information and advice offered here, but it really all comes down to:

"Breathing and Bumper Stickers"

Here are the reasons why I believe in this bumper sticker regarding good speech:

Reason #1: Technique is built on the basics.

Reason #2: True forward momentum is both physical and mental.

Reason #3: Relaxation and clarity equal confidence.

There are many more reasons, and even much more detailed reasons, but most listeners can only absorb three at a time. So you need to make them clear and you need to make them count. Notice that reasons one, two, and three answer the questions "What do you mean?" and "Why do you believe this is true?"

Returning to the theme (of the crime). Your listeners are always looking to understand the connections between information and concepts. They want to connect the dots! Without a clear message or bumper sticker, your listeners don't know what they're looking for. Your bumper sticker becomes that recurring theme that keeps popping up, reminding your listeners that everything you're saying serves a single purpose. They become intrigued by the unfolding of the story that is in front of them.

Your bumper sticker is also the theme that will not leave you—even when you are processing new information and considering another's perspective. Your clarity will be the forward momentum of your thoughts, perceived as passion and commitment.

Additionally, even if your listeners were to "zone out" after the first ten seconds of your presentation, they would still have an idea of what you came there to say. But trust me, they won't zone out if you follow through on the discipline of discovering and using bumper stickers.

Tall tales. All important speaking is storytelling. The stories you choose tell a lot about you. Of course, they are based on life experiences, but they can be crafted to have relevant, adaptable beginnings and consistent endings, or buttons. Good storytelling requires a clear perspective and practice. It is amazing how similar your business and personal stories can be when you know how you want to describe yourself. Once you realize what to look for, each day will bring new opportunities to craft compelling narratives that connect with people and make strong impressions.

Stories that define you. We all know a good story when we hear it. The qualities of intrigue, balance, and closure are all present. The story doesn't ramble. It gets to the point—with a little embellishment. Pumping your stories up with a little comedy or drama goes a long way toward making them interesting and relevant. Even tall tales have a foundation that is authentic and true. It is in the retelling that they grow into truly sensational narratives. You definitely have the license to "enhance" your stories.

You begin by recalling the life experiences that you feel define you. What are your best qualities? What experiences from your life are examples of you displaying those qualities? Even out of the ordinary and outlandish stories work because you were there and you either participated or you observed.

The difference between a tall tale and your story is that you were really there. You have the advantage of being able to communicate what it felt like to live through the experience you are describing. Give yourself permission to go there. Remember, it's not considered bragging if your listeners can relate to the feeling at the core of the story.

The material world. There are so many sources of material for a good story. You can base a story on a real-life experience—for example, stories in the distant past, stories from the recent past, things that happened today, work-related stories, stories about having fun, or school-related stories. Even though you might be talking about the past, relate the story to the present. This is one way of grounding your story's relevance. Make sure that you spread your stories out. In other words, don't focus all of your stories on one era of your life—childhood memories, college stories, or work experiences. You don't want any one period of your life to sound as if it was your glory days.

If you're having a difficult time generating stories, consider these topics to spark some ideas: the inconvenience of travel, the joy of experiencing something for the first time, trying a new restaurant, a break from the usual routine, amusing confessions, embarrassing moments, and your favorite vacation memory.

Funny observations or complaints work well, but only if you can deliver them in a self-deprecating way with no bitterness. Stay away from complaints that really sound like complaining; for example, your job, your relationships, and more. Stay completely away from health issues. The great news is that most of your stories can be used in almost any interaction. Remember that the raw material of any story has to matter to you. Even a good story that you've heard can work if it resonates with you and you can communicate that connection.

Arts and crafts. As much as there is an art to the telling of a good story, the foundation is the well-crafted story itself. Good stories are crafted over time usually by telling them over and over again. If you're seeking some help in this area, then you probably are not comfortable with the trial-and-error approach to honing your stories on the fly. There is some behind-the-scenes work you can do before you put your stories on display for all to see.

Once you have chosen material that matters to you and is worth telling, practice recounting the experience out loud until you discover the reason for telling it. Much like a good joke, there should always be a punchline or revelation at the end of the story called a "button." In the same way you discover the bumper sticker of a presentation, the button grows out of the reason why you're telling the story.

Good beginnings to stories can be crafted from a good metaphor. Saying your experience was like a universally understood metaphor is the easiest way to set up your stories. After all, that's what a metaphor is for! They help to frame any story in relevance and allow your listeners to find their connection to your experience as it unfolds in the telling.

Weaving 101. The secret to being able to smoothly and effectively insert your stories into a conversation or a presentation is to edit them in three lengths. The long-form, three-minute version of a story is fine for intimate conversations where there is time and need for increased details. The ninety-second version works best when you are holding the spotlight during a presentation or a meeting. The thirty-second version is extremely useful during a lively group conversation where everyone is expected to and wants to participate. At first, this may sound far too calculated and not at all spontaneous. Remember that you are using your stories as tools to promote yourself and your ideas.

When you know what your stories are, you can look for openings in the conversation to fit them in. You will get better at the process. How can you look for an opening when you are not aware of what you're looking for? Certain key words or topics of discussion will begin to trigger your recognition that you have a story that fits. It feels as if you're hashtagging a tweet on Twitter. What are the possible connections? How can I spark some interest? These connections become the potential segues that you look for.

This approach may sound very simple and obvious. The problem is that many individuals never take the time to think about preparing themselves to truly succeed as a conversationalist or as a presenter.

Polish as you go. Stories always get better in the retelling. So, don't hold back. Practice telling them whenever you can. Don't wait for an important conversation, event, or presentation to be the motivation that makes you become a great storyteller. When the spotlight is on you, even for just a moment or two, go for it! Your stories are as unique as your life experience. Focus on the material that will best describe you in an authentic way. The wonderful thing about working on the craft of storytelling is that it gets easier as you do it. Consistent storytelling will help you to see the relevance of almost any new life experience. Once you know how to put a good story together, even the new stories can start to sound very interesting, polished, and effective.

12

Fear and Loathing
Fearless Tricks

All speech for business is public speaking. To fear and loathe public speaking is to put an unnecessary ceiling on your career. This fear is unnecessary, but it feels very real and very intense. It should because it is real. The way you perceive things is subjective, but there are some very real forces that are present whenever you find yourself in a public speaking scenario. The good news is that, once again, all business communications are a form of public speaking. That means you have many smaller opportunities to prepare yourself for the big rush of a presentation or a large event. You just need to look at it the right way and practice, practice, practice!

The three-headed monster. There are three forces at work whenever any individual finds themselves in the public speaking spotlight: the energy of attention, the sense of judgment, and the fear of consequences. Most people lump them all together and call it "nerves." That nervous feeling is actually a reaction to the sudden awareness of the three-headed monster coming toward you. It sounds like a fantasy, but these forces are real—and ever present. In order to tame the beast, you must look at the three heads separately.

The energy of attention is the strongest of the three, and it is actually the trigger for the other two. Whenever you speak to even one person you can feel the energy of their presence and they can feel yours. Increasing the number of people you are addressing increases that level of attention, or focus. It is a very real condition, just like the weather. You can't change it, and you can't ignore it. But you can see it for what it is. The energy of attention is the main reason why there is always a feeling of excitement when you speak to a group. The larger the group the higher the level of attention. If you are uncomfortable with the energy, you will probably find yourself feeling nervousness.

The second force that suddenly enters a public speaker's awareness is the sense of judgment. The word *judgment* itself often gets a bad rap. No one likes judgmental people, and a final judgment sounds so ominous and well, final. But we use our judgment in so many ways to make good and important decisions everyday. Judgment is also the sense that your listeners use to determine if you are indeed "driving the bus" and if they are comfortable following along. So, when all eyes are on you and you feel as if everyone is judging you, they are! It is what they are supposed to do, and it is, in fact, what you want them to do. Acceptance of this reality goes a long way to helping you see things for what they are.

The last head on the monster is the fear of consequences. This force is not as strong as the first two, but it is constantly there in the back of your mind. It can be a general feeling of wanting to make good impressions and taking advantage of this opportunity to advance your career. On a personal level, you may also fear stumbling and letting yourself down once again. Your mind can slide very quickly into the cloud of consequences if you don't recognize the triggers that push you there. It can happen in the blink of an eye if you're not prepared.

Getting wet. The energy of attention is the primary trigger for the nervous feeling so many individuals experience. I mentioned earlier that when two people speak they both feel the energy of each other's attention. When the number of participants changes, the ratio of the energy of attention changes too. Add four more people to the mix and you will feel five times the energy of attention coming toward you when it's your turn to speak. Conversely, your attention toward each listener has now dropped to one-fifth of what it was during the one-on-one conversation. That hardly seems fair! Knowing what is happening in these types of scenarios goes a long way to explaining what you perceive and making sense of it.

Worrying about whether you are going to feel this energy imbalance coming toward you in those crucial first seconds is where the fear develops. Fear is anxiety over what you think is going to happen. When you know what will happen, you can better prepare yourself. It's comparable to standing at the edge of a lake and worrying about whether you will get wet when you jump in. You can choose not to jump in. But when you have to give a speech or presentation, you are going in the lake!

The scientific word for acceptance of circumstances is *habituation*. Becoming accustomed to anything will happen over time. Because the rush of energy in the opening moments of public speaking is so sudden and overwhelming, your body reacts with a fight-or-flight response. You can condition yourself to lessen this response if you recognize what is going on, and you can ride the initial wave of energy.

Go time! Now that you know the cause of your nervousness, you will be able to focus your mind on what really is and isn't going on. That's all well and good. But how do you stop your body from repeating the same behavior over and over again? The fight-or-flight response causes tightness in the body, a clenching of the diaphragm muscle, and shallow breathing. By focusing on your diaphragm muscle, you will ease the tension and increase your inhalation of air that is so vital to being able to speak and move things forward.

Here is a simple exercise that will increase the amount of control you have over your diaphragm muscle. Inhale slowly over four seconds. Then exhale even more slowly. The amount of time that an individual can exhale will vary. Try to allow all of the air in your lungs to slowly escape. Once you have reached that point, resist the urge to breathe in too quickly. Wait for three to four seconds as if you are calmly sitting at the bottom of a pool before you take a long, welcomed inhalation. This is the key to the exercise and the key to your relaxation and control. Now slowly repeat this exercise, extending the length of your exhalation. Make sure you are always attempting to squeeze out the last remaining air in your lungs. As you repeat this exercise you should feel an increased sense of calm and relaxation.

Focusing on breathing will also serve as your primary source of forward momentum when speaking. It will give you the strong start that you need. The first ten seconds are critical. This is the time that you can establish that you are in charge, but not in an adversarial way. Remember, the majority of listeners are empathetic and want to hear what you have to contribute.

Finding Neverland. Don't let the true nature of public speaking surprise you. Far too many people lose their way, wondering, "Why is this happening again?" You need to practice recognizing the forces that are at work in less stressful situations. Participating at an impromptu meeting can be a good practice ground. Remember that all business communications contain an aspect of public speaking. The reduced pressure of speaking at a meeting will allow you to monitor your reactions and get your mind and body used to being more at ease with the circumstances that surround you. Habituation takes recognition, practice, and time. Public speaking does not have to be a once a month or a once a year roll of the dice. If you can work to eliminate the element of surprise, your odds for success will greatly increase.

The energy of attention, the sense of judgment, and the fear of consequences are all real. Together they create an unstoppable wave that you need to recognize and prepare for in any business setting. This reality can certainly compound any lack of confidence you may have in your speech technique. On the flip side, learning to ride the wave can increase the power of your message exponentially. It may sound as if you're playing with fire, but you have no choice. Your comfort, your confidence, and your career depend on your ability to deal with the fear and to harness the power of public speaking.

All in. Staying grounded is the key to surviving and flourishing in the first fifteen seconds of any public-speaking scenario. You are expected to project outward while so many forces are moving in on you! Practice relying on your body as you prepare for what you know is coming. Studies have shown that body language accounts for over 50 percent of any message you are trying to convey. It consists of confident posture, supportive gestures, and appropriate eye contact and facial expressions. All of these communication tools should be used to the fullest! Receptive body language sends the message that you are committed to the ideas and words you're saying. More importantly, it gives you the sensation of being fully connected. Speech should always be a full-body experience—even when talking on the phone! Gesturing and facial expressions definitely have a positive effect on the sound of your voice. Your body language has the power to add subtle, unspoken nuance to everything you say. When you lack good body language, you can only tell half the story.

The magical speaker. To anyone struggling with their public-speaking abilities, good speakers seem like magicians. They grab your attention and hold it. They never seem to be at a loss for words. They take their time, as if they should be listened to. They always seem to know in what direction they want to take the conversation or topic. The way they carry themselves oozes confidence. They are never brash in their delivery, but their message definitely comes through loud and clear. You trust that what they have to say is thoughtful and important enough to be heard and considered. They really sound as if they mean it, and they make it look seamless and easy. So, how do they achieve this sleight of hand?

The speakers we admire use all of their body language to engage their listeners. They do this either intuitively or through years of practice. Gesturing, eye contact, facial expressions, and posture are all in perfect balance. This may seem like too much to think about when you're nervous and under pressure to deliver. The good news is that that they are all connected. Once you start to integrate one type of body language, your use of the rest will also improve.

Exercises for recognizing body language in use. I always say, "Learn from the best." Go to the Internet and find a video of a speaker you admire or simply visit TED Talks to view a wide array of various speakers. Focus on just one aspect of body language that your chosen speaker has mastered, such as gesturing. After a few minutes, change your focus to facial expressions. The subtle differences in the body language of speakers are what make them unique. You may not be comfortable replicating everything you see, but at least you will be aware of how important body language is to a speaker's overall presentation. Remember, it's not the words that they're saying, it is the body language that they are using that makes them appear authentic and confident.

When you feel confident that you can spot and separate speech behavior, try observing body language utilization in a business meeting setting. Ideally, you should pick a meeting at which you have limited responsibility to speak yourself. Watch the other speakers very closely. You will recognize that the best speakers know how to use their bodies to full advantage. Watch for these "tricks of the trade" and then start to use them yourself.

What's holding you back? Wouldn't it be wonderful if you could speak as easily in a meeting as you do sitting around with friends and family? So, what's holding you back from achieving this level of comfort when speaking about business? The key to increasing your comfort is in your consistent use of positive body language.

There can be many reasons for overlooking or even avoiding the use of body language when you speak. You may have been told that gesturing makes you look nervous, too much eye contact can be creepy, in business you should always keep it professional and stoic, or always keep things close to the vest in business and in life. I am here to tell you that *you* are holding you back!

First, let me dispel the notion that speaking in a professional manner means being ultraconservative in your delivery. That never feels good, and it is probably the behavior that is holding you back the most. Now, there is such a thing as talking too much; we all recognize when a speaker is gesturing too much. It is not the amount that matters as much as the commitment. Gesturing fully shows that you are ready, willing, and able to share your perspective. A committed speaker sends the message that they are worth listening to. You will definitely hold your listener's attention longer and your storytelling will be more compelling. You will also have the sensation of feeling more physically engaged in the act of speaking.

Some very common obstacles to expressing your thoughts clearly are: fear of judgment, fear of consequences, and trying to match the pace of your mouth with your mind. A combination of some or all of these potential obstacles can make clear communication very difficult. It's not that the ideas aren't there; it's that you're worrying about too many things that you can't control. The problem is that you are being distracted by thinking that you should try to control them. The reality is that there is judgment, there are consequences, and your mouth simply cannot keep up with your mind. It is important to clear the way for clarity. Focus on the things that you can control: your breathing, your perspective, and your sense of commitment through the use of body language.

Exercises for handling obstacles. All speech for business is a form of public speaking. There are a lot of things happening all at once when you find yourself in the role of public speaker. If any of them are consistently holding you back, they are obstacles. However, just like the weather, they are merely circumstances that you have to deal with. That doesn't mean that you are a victim or that you should do nothing. Try using strong, supportive body language to push through the circumstance of judgment.

Take a deep breath and say the following phrase, gesturing with both hands outstretched on the word *matter*.

"It doesn't *matter* how they judge me."

Take another deep breath and shrug your shoulders on the word *let*.
"*Let* them judge."
Take another deep breath and gesture with hands again on the word *do*.
"They're going to *do* it anyway."

You may think that you are putting too much focus on the problem. What you are actually doing is learning to habituate with one circumstance of public speaking. You are learning to put this sense of empowerment into your body by using strong body language.

Speaking these words with deliberate gestures is essential to keeping your mind from racing when the public speaking moment is at hand. After practicing the exercise above several times, try substituting the first three short sentences, or phrases, of your speech or presentation. Your body will be reminded of your recognition of the circumstance of judgment and will connect what you're saying to your acceptance of the circumstance. Body language keeps you grounded, relaxed, and in control when you need it the most.

The mental/physical connection. Many of my business clients explain to me that they know the subject matter of their presentation or speech very well but they still tend to choke up when speaking their ideas to others. They describe it as a sensation of hesitating to consider every single word that flows out of their mouths. They recognize the need to get out of their heads, or to let at least a few of their good ideas out in a coherent fashion. Most of the time what they are experiencing is the disconnect between their minds and their bodies.

Your body can send the signal to your mind that you are either standing still or moving forward. The signal that your speech should flow forward is created through active use of body language—more specifically, gesturing.

Lack of body language awareness can be a major kink in the hose that allows your spoken ideas to flow. You know what it feels like to be in the flow, and you know what it feels like when you're not. Body language that is stiff, held back, or passive can actually cause you to deliver your ideas in a choppy and disjointed manner. The body and mind connection is very strong and needs to be used everyday. Effective speech is a full-body experience.

Gesturing not only supports everything you say, but it is also your lifeline when your mind begins to race and your negative thoughts start to get the best of you. By reconnecting to your body with breath, you will be allowing the words to flow.

Exercises for connected speech. For someone who is not accustomed to gesturing, this all might seem as if it is "over the top." It will seem as if it is just too much. You have to break through your reluctance to gesture by pushing yourself a bit in practice to get to a place where you are comfortable and relaxed when gesturing. Trust me when I tell you that it will get better with time.

First of all, you have to speak slowly enough to allow for connection to your impulses. Breathing deliberately is the simplest way to both slow down your rate of speech and connect to your body.

Use these sentences to build a strong body connection. Take a deep, supportive breath and gesture freely, landing your gesture on the underlined word. Make sure you hold your gesture in place while taking your preparatory breath for the next sentence.

"<u>That's</u> where we find ourselves today." (Hold your gesture while taking a deep breath.)

"<u>I</u> believe our position is very clear." (Hold your gesture while taking a deep breath.)

"There is <u>definitely</u> room for further discussion." (Hold your gesture; take a deep breath.)

"We don't <u>have</u> the luxury of time." (Hold your gesture; take a deep breath.)

"<u>All</u> of your concerns will be addressed." (Hold your gesture; take a deep breath.)

"I'd like to <u>share</u> my insights on the matter." (Hold your gesture.)

Repeat this exercise speaking the sentences in reverse order, from bottom to top.

You need to develop a consistent feeling of forward momentum in your body. This will also project a sense of forward momentum onto the things you say. More importantly, you need to rely on the physical side of speech to rescue you when the pressure is on. Learn how to connect and use your body through gesturing.

In door/out door. Biofeedback consists of signals from your body. These are the sensations that help you monitor your vocal condition. They can also be reminders of your level of commitment, passion, and authenticity. Sensations that you feel and perceptions that you project can be one in the same, but you need to give yourself permission to think and act this way. This may seem easy enough to understand conceptually, but it can be very difficult to execute consistently. Speech habits are very ingrained human behavior. That's why practicing actionable steps is so important.

For better or worse, public speaking moments come and go so quickly. The first ten seconds of any speech or presentation sets the tone for whether you will struggle uphill for the rest of your time in the spotlight or whether you will convince yourself and your listeners to trust that you are in charge. You are not waiting for validation; you are creating the reality using body-language tools. You really are convincing yourself first and then projecting that sense of commitment to your listeners. You have to take it in before you can give it out. Your comfort in using your body effectively is what brings confidence to the delivery of your message.

Exercises for confident gesturing. A gesture can land on whatever word feels natural to you. Allow yourself to gesture in an uninhibited way by imagining that you're speaking the sentences of this exercise to a friend. Hold your gesture long after you're done speaking, and recognize the energy and intention that stays within your body. Remember, relaxation leads to comfort, which leads to confidence.

Speak this sentence using a downward gesture, with palms up in an imploring manner.

"When will we have an answer?"

Gesture inward (toward your chest) to personalize this next message.

"These are things I need to know."

Deliver the following sentence with an outstretched gesture of inclusion

"We have all seen this before."

Use a downward gesture, with palms down in a negative manner when speaking this sentence.

"This is not what I signed up for."

Speak the next sentence pointing upward as if informing or quoting.

"There is one thing we forgot."

Point outward in a demanding manner when delivering this sentence.
  "We did it anyway."

The intention we recognize within our bodies can be conveyed to others.
What we feel we can make others feel. This is the in door/out door technique in a nutshell. Trust in the sensation of commitment and confidence
that strong, supportive body language will give you.

And the voice will follow. The rhythm and the pitch of your voice is
what is known as your *intonation.* Many people will often refer to the tone
of their voice. Your body language can definitely have an effect on the
tone of your voice. This is especially important to remember when speaking on the phone. Whether you're running the call, speaking one on one,
or sharing your perspective with a group, starting strong and maintaining
good forward momentum are critical phone skills. Forward momentum
should not be confused with pace. Speaking too quickly can be distracting
and hard to process. You need to be connected to your breath and your
body so that you have the time and the support needed to let the words
flow. You need to gesture as if the individuals you're speaking to are actually in the room looking at you. The more you gesture the more interesting
and authentic you will sound. This approach will give you the confidence
and sense of authority needed to be truly persuasive.

Exercises for varying intonation. Simply change the word in the sentence where you choose to place your gesture and your emphasis. Take a
deep breath and allow your impulses to guide you to a different gesture
each time. Notice how your intention and intonation also change.

"<u>I</u> think we all have a responsibility to never let this happen again."
"I <u>think</u> we all have a responsibility to never let this happen again."
"I think <u>we</u> all have a responsibility to never let this happen again."
"I think we <u>all</u> have a responsibility to never let this happen again."
"I think we all <u>have</u> a responsibility to never let this happen again."
"I think we all have a <u>responsibility</u> to never let this happen again."
"I think we all have a responsibility to <u>never</u> let this happen again."
"I think we all have a responsibility to never <u>let</u> this happen again."
"I think we all have a responsibility to never let <u>this</u> happen again."
"I think we all have a responsibility to never let this <u>happen</u> again."

Try taking this concept a step further by walking around the room at a measured pace. It's rare that you would use this technique in person, but over the phone you should use any advantage possible to generate a sense of energy in your delivery. This approach will increase your willingness to gesture more freely.

As I live and breathe! Breathing is a very effective form of body language when executed deliberately. It is also the way to integrate gesturing into your everyday communications. Gesturing should not be something you turn on only when you're public speaking for business. The everyday integration of this technique will make it so much easier to execute when the pressure is on. Neither you nor your listeners will feel as if you're "putting on a show." The idea is to get to the place where you feel relaxed and grounded in your body.

You have to give yourself the opportunity to know what it feels like to experience the freedom of overcoming this common physical obstacle. Nobody said it would be easy or that it would feel great right away. Speech behavior, like any other human behavior, is initially very hard to change. That's why so many people give up while still early in the process of increasing their speaking comfort. It isn't easy to go "all in" when you are unsure of what you're doing or why you're doing it.

Exercises for integrated body language. When sitting around talking with friends, no one ever holds back their gesturing or even thinks about their body language and breathing. It is the increased awareness of judgment when speaking for business that can stifle how connected you are to your impulses and to your authentic nature. Forcing yourself to push through the initial wave of uncertainty requires awareness, practice, and discipline. You need to become a student of your own body language and learn to use it at even the most everyday opportunities.

Here are some scenarios that you may recognize. They all occur outside of the workplace. Give yourself the chance to explore and experiment.

1: Be aware of your body language when ordering at a lunch counter or a coffee shop. These can be very loud environments. In fact, listeners truly rely on body language to clearly understand your message when ordering.

2: You can practice facial expressions and gesturing when catching up with a neighbor over the weekend. You will undoubtedly be talking about funny moments and frustrating moments. Either way, the subject matter will mean something to you. Follow your impulses and go for it!

3: Make sure you practice the recalling of how your day went with your spouse. Stating the facts of your day is never enough. Sharing the experience through body language is the way to connect.

4: You may find yourself talking to your insurance company (or a similar company) over the phone. You need to be very clear, definitive, and, at times, demanding. Your body language will give you that forward momentum to get your point across.

5: Finally, if you really want to raise the stakes, try talking politics with a relative. Agreeing to disagree can be much more satisfying if you know you actually have an ulterior motive. You will be using the heated discussion to practice being all in!

I like all of these communication scenarios because it is easy to get caught up in them; you don't have the time to think about holding yourself back. When it's your turn to make a point, let your gestures be full but not necessarily effusive. By connecting to your body through gesturing your intonation will naturally vary enough to convey the appropriate level of commitment to the words you're speaking. The goal is to understand the connectivity of good vocal balance and then transfer that feeling over to business communications where the perceived stakes are much higher. Your vocal balance is your public speaking lifeline!

13

Annoying Habits
Habit-Changing Shortcuts

The daily repetition of speech can create some less-than-desirable patterns. Listeners pick up on them right away, but speakers are not always so aware. The use of filler words and sounds, speaking in a monotone, and "up speak" are the most common patterns. They sabotage the delivery of every message because they make your listeners pay attention to how you are saying something, not what you're saying. Undetected, some speech patterns can go from being a mere distraction to being the cause of negative perceptions.

The obvious ones. You may actually catch yourself falling into speech patterns that can leave negative impressions. The obvious bad speech habits are the ones you can actually hear yourself doing. Luckily, they can all be corrected by making physical adjustments to your overall speech technique. Once again, it is not "all in your head." Undesirable speech patterns are not necessarily an indication of your true persona. Recognize the need for change and make adjustments to your delivery. The pattern will not go away on its own.

It's like, well, um, uh-h-h. These are examples of filler words and sounds that should be used as little as possible in any speaking for business. They make you sound less confident and even less intelligent. All spoken sounds are created when breath is exhaled from the body. Therefore, the integration of more deliberate breath inhalation is the best way to correct this annoying habit. There can't be any unwanted sounds when you are actively inhaling. The bonus is that the body language of deliberate breathing sends a visual message of thoughtfulness, pose, and maturity.

The monotone drone. Speaking with very little variation in your rhythm or pitch is what is commonly referred to as a monotone. The usual association is that the speaker is bored with what they are saying. This very quickly leads to disinterest on the part of listeners because it never sounds like the overall delivery is ever going to change. Most monotone speakers barely move their mouths when speaking. Therefore, their vowel space is truncated and small. Voices have the opportunity to relax when speaking large, long vowels with good vowel space. Treating all of the vowel sounds in exactly the same way leads to a tight, narrow band of expression. Add to this that the ability to start and stop and change rhythms is also controlled by your breath. The end result is a lack of confidence in being able to change the pitch, rhythm, and melody of your voice. This ineffective speech habit loses listeners very quickly even though you know your subject matter inside and out! A monotone voice is always rooted in the body. Focus on your breathing and vowel space as you breathe new life into the sound of your voice.

The runaway train. Speaking too quickly can get you in trouble. It never sounds good . . . and you probably know it. Negative impressions can grow out of not knowing how to slow down or how to come to a stop. Whether you're in a conversation or giving a presentation, reasonable gaps have to be taken to allow your listeners to process what you're saying. Accelerated speech can make people think you are either trying to overwhelm them with thoughts and information, get the interaction over with as quickly as possible, or that you're really nervous. It can actually show a great deal of disrespect toward your listeners.

Give yourself permission to adopt a slower speech pattern by integrating deliberate breathing into your cadence. Hold onto your gestures as a way to maintain unspoken continuity while you are breathing. These actions will send the message that you are truly considering your words and that they mean something to you. Projecting authority as a speaker depends on your ability to slow down. In a business world where we are told that time is money, the real currency is communicating clearly at a poised and measured pace.

Under the radar. Some annoying habits start out as a good idea but then change over time. Friendly facial expressions, lively intonation, and excited delivery can lead to repetitive behavior that can send the wrong message to your listeners. You need to take your technique in for a tune-up every once in a while to keep it distraction free.

The dread of spread. I wrote in earlier chapters about the negative effect of spread on your ability to articulate correctly and easily. The constant smile that comes with spread can be perceived as a speaker being disingenuous in their delivery. Although smiling is a friendly facial expression, too much smiling is, well, too much sometimes. It can develop from a well-intentioned desire to be affable, cooperative, and respectfully interested in another's perspective. Couple that with overarticulation and a lack of breath support and you have the potential for spread.

Tightness and even pain in the upper cheek muscles can be an indicator that you are speaking with spread. You may also sense a lack of trust on the part of your listeners. If you notice they are not occasionally smiling or nodding along with the points you're making, you may be a victim of your own spread. On the other hand, if they are constantly smiling along with you, they may be guilty of spread too!

Up speak. The melody of your voice matters, especially at the end of your sentences. Up speak is a pattern of speech where most of your sentences end on a higher pitch. Therefore, they sound like they are going up rather than ending down in a definitive way. Everything starts to sound as if it is being delivered as a question and not as a strong statement of fact or opinion. The majority of your sentences should end on a lower pitch. Even most rhetorical questions end in a definitive manner by going down. Up speak usually develops from a need to connect information together. The speaker wants to make sure the listener knows that there is more to come and doesn't want to lose their attention. Very often the speaker is guilty of constantly using run on, compound sentences that try to include too much information and not enough clear perspective.

Limited breathing and breath support, especially when you're nervous, will make the problem even worse. It is very hard to end a sentence with authority when you're running out of air. Remember that any presentation or conversation is a series of statements. Allow your listeners to connect those statements together. Up speak will make you sound unsure of yourself, as if you are asking for some sort of validation for the message you are delivering. It erodes the sense of trust that you need from your listeners.

Say it again, Sam. Speaking the majority of your sentences with the same intonation, or cadence, gets very repetitive and boring. The same holds true for repeating the same gesture over and over again. This habit tends to increase when the physical stress of public speaking creeps in. Being able to change your gestures is also the key to changing up the intonation of your speech. To check on whether you have developed the habit of repetition, use a two-to-three-minute portion of your presentation that you are very familiar with. Speak in front of a mirror while coming up with at least six different gestures without repeating a single gesture. You will probably discover that you have a "go to" gesture that has a tendency to repeat. Break down the small sample of your presentation sentence by sentence and discipline yourself to not repeat a gesture. The good news is that there are unlimited gestures! You have to learn to tap into your own sense of creative and supportive gesturing and become comfortable with using it. There is a direct connection between varied gesturing and varied intonation. The result is that you will be a more interesting and compelling speaker.

Missing the train. There are several factors that can cause you to lose your train of thought. It can be the result of not realizing that your mind and your mouth move at different speeds. Think of your thoughts and your spoken words as two conveyor belts moving at totally different speeds. Obviously, your mind moves at a much faster pace than your mouth. In order for both to work efficiently and effectually, you have to trust that you can speak at a nice, steady pace while you focus on what you want to say next. Taking the time to breathe and gesture deliberately will give you those precious, extra nanoseconds your mind needs to make the connection to your thoughts that will then become spontaneous speech.

Trying to deliver too much information is like focusing on each individual step of a journey. It can cause you to lose your way. You need to develop guideposts along the way that will keep you on the right course. Clearly defining your guideposts, or bullet points, not only serves to point you in the right direction, it will also give you freedom to be spontaneous, answer questions, and enjoy the scenery without the fear of falling off the path. Be careful that you don't create too many bullet points; remember that most listeners have a three-idea limit. Use this knowledge to your advantage as you plan your trip!

Forgetting to create and practice segues between spoken ideas can be yet another trip wire. Memorization is not as important as preparation. Recognizing the major ideas and the connectivity between them will allow your listeners to process right along with you. Most presenters are not aware of how important it is to speak their presentation out loud. You need to know what it feels like to deliver your words. The sudden surprise of hearing your own voice actually deliver your words can cause you to lose your way and potentially fall off the rails.

Blocking the flow. The majority of bad speech habits are rooted in the body, but they have a cumulative effect on the mind. They block your ability to let your spoken ideas flow. If the condition persists long enough, you will begin to habituate with that feeling and start to consider yourself to be shy, or just a good listener but not a good talker. You have to recognize bad speech habits for what they are and then take the necessary steps to counteract their effect on your technique. You need to be aware of what could be holding you back and giving people the wrong impression of who you are and what you're trying to say.

14

Connecting the Dots
Executive Presence Shortcuts

So many businesspeople are looking for ways to increase their Executive Presence. The term is thrown around as being the highest level of business behavior to be emulated. But what does it really mean to have it? Everyone knows when they see and hear someone exude Executive Presence. It's not just good grooming or fashion sense, and even highly developed intelligence or street smarts are not the key. When people look to you as a leader, they have to recognize that the way you walk and talk represents controlled forward momentum. Ideally, you want to project that you are going somewhere and you are confident enough to take your listeners with you. Before you can connect with people on this level you need to recognize and trust that all of the various aspects of your speech technique are in balance and support each other. Your ability to execute simple and subtle changes to the pattern of your delivery depends on that trust. By connecting the dots you will be stepping into the mental zone that others experience when they are projecting their own Executive Presence. You need to develop this ability on a daily basis. Expecting your technique to be polished and effective only when on full display is like expecting to play golf at a championship level while only playing once a week. You need to connect the dots everyday!

Recognizing the balance. Vocal balance is a feeling of being well supported with forward momentum and relaxation. It is your vocal apparatus working at peak efficiency. The ease and fluidity of your body language becomes the gauge that indicates your increased level of comfort and confidence. The ability to start and stop and add inflection becomes second nature. You can adjust the projection of your voice based on a variety of circumstances. Your pace is measured when driving home a point and sweeping when caught up in the excitement and passion of your message. Knowing how to connect your breathing, your gesturing, your intonation, and your projection will give you the sensation of being in balance. None of these aspects of your speech technique are isolated. A good public speaker connects all of them together seamlessly.

Overwhelmed to meet you. I make it a habit to always try to learn from the best. When you are in the presence of a really good speaker, look for the speech skills they are using. Recognize their breathing, their posture, gesturing, facial expressions, and measured pace. At first it may seem as if they're doing nothing out of the ordinary. But when you break it down, you will notice that their fundamental technique is smooth, solid, and connected. All of the parts work together in a cohesive presentation. Don't just shrink away when you compare yourself to them; learn from the speakers you admire. When you know what to look for, it can be quite an education. Discipline yourself to look for the following (in no particular order):

Good speakers use deliberate breathing.
Good speakers gesture fully and completely.
Good speakers vary their intonation: pitches are high and low; rhythms are fast and slow.
Good speakers have a cadence that is deliberate and sweeping.
Good speakers understand the importance of eye contact: appropriately balanced in small groups and inclusive in large groups.
Good speakers use bumper stickers that are clear and concise.
Good speakers return to their bumper stickers often for emphasis.

These crucial aspects of good speech technique can be hard to notice when a speaker has mastered the art of putting them all together. Yes, sometimes the magician is so good that, even though you know the details of the sleight of hand, you still get lost in the brilliance of the show.

Ride the wave. Don't ever discount what vocal comfort can do for your confidence and your sense of presence in a conversation, meeting, or presentation. Being physically prepared is the foundation for being mentally and emotionally prepared for whatever challenges may come. Many will refer to this perception as Executive Presence. The feeling can be summed up with the phrase, "I've got this." The level of confidence at which you can deliver this message will determine your Executive Presence. It begins in the body. That's what makes it ooze with authenticity. Connecting to your body connects you to your true perspective and allows you to walk the walk and talk the talk.

Hearing your body. Hearing your body means understanding your body's responses and not allowing them to consciously or unconsciously hold you back or give you cause to pause. The perceived freedom needed for spontaneous speech is actually based in the support of your controlled breathing. Your confidence will grow as you learn to recognize whether an obstacle is mental or physical and whether you are dealing with a true or an imposed perception. Learning to separate your feelings into thoughts and sensations helps to mitigate the downward spiral that can begin with only one habitual response. You need to develop methods of actively catching yourself before you free fall. Deliberately controlling your breath when your physical response is to go to shallow breathing is the crucial first step. You need to stay connected to your body when you feel unsure and your mind wants to run! Gesturing fully will increase your sense of forward momentum, and it will project the same to your listeners.

The ten-thousand-hour shortcut. There is a widely known theory that it takes about ten thousand hours of practice to become a master at something. However, the way you practice can reduce the time it takes to achieve your goals. Performers know that each performance hour is equal to about four practice hours. By recognizing that all speech for business is a form of public speaking you can treat all of your interactions as performances. These are opportunities to follow good discipline and figure out how to execute what works. Don't be afraid to put yourself on the spot and maintain a high level of focus and concentration. Now that you know what to look for you can challenge yourself and make adjustments that directly affect how efficiently you communicate. The really good news is that every time you interact you will be receiving continuous feedback from your listeners. This is the perfect scenario for achieving faster results.

Exploring the edges. You can boldly set off to explore and experiment with intonation and gesturing knowing that you have a base camp of fundamentally sound speech technique to return to. When you know how to start and stop and how to push forward in a relaxed way, you have the tools to take on whatever might lie ahead. Truly dynamic speakers have a sense of knowing where they want to get to while still sharing the experience of arriving there for the first time. Don't stop challenging yourself to be more committed, more relaxed, and ultimately, more compelling.

Powerful persuasion. Moving from a place of fear to a position of persuasion requires touching several different layers of how you understand your speech technique. Once you have determined and removed the physical obstacles, precise preparation will allow you to share your unique perspective openly and efficiently with your listeners. The true goal is to simply convince them that you are ready, willing, and able to share that perspective. Your listeners will always decide for themselves how they will step into the framework you have presented. This is engagement at the highest level with impactful results.

The gravitas (in all of us). Your words carry importance if you say they do. Which is not to say that you should always be serious and solemn in your delivery. Being funny and even silly is important too! In regard to speech, gravitas refers to a level of commitment. It is the perception that you mean what you say. If you are truly filtering your spoken thoughts through your perspective, they will matter to you. Be empowered by this sense of importance, especially when you are speaking due to a work obligation. Others may not always agree with your point of view. Infusing your perspective will inject authenticity into the words you say, leading to the trust that is so crucial to developing business relationships.

I know that you know that I know. Don't mistakenly think that you have the entire length of your presentation or meeting to make an impression on your listeners. Positive impressions are established almost immediately. They are then reinforced consistently throughout your talk. Be clear right away. And don't wait for validation when speaking. Make it clear that you are the one driving the bus and that you know what you want to convey. Getting your listeners to agree with your point of view is not your most important job. They will decide for themselves whether or not they are in agreement with you. They will probably debate you about your point of view later. So, give them a clear message to work with. You may not "know it all," but you should definitely know what you want. It may sound selfish or even opportunistic, but embracing your perspective and then saying it clearly are refreshing qualities to develop and possess.

Master of the pause. Any good speech coach (and any good musician, for that matter) will tell you that the very best know how to "play the silence in between." Becoming a "Master of the Pause" in speech requires good diaphragm regulation, synchronized gesturing, and confidence in applied inflection. Deliberate breathing is the difference maker. The interesting thing is that listeners really do pay attention to a deliberate gap in your spoken words. They perk up, anticipating what you will say next. The subtle use of the pause is a wonderful way to keep your listeners' attention and add gravitas to your message. Maintaining attention requires controlling the gap of silence so that you don't look like a "deer in the headlights." The perception should be that you are giving your listeners space to process what you're saying and make a connection to the concepts you are conveying. Pausing effectively requires that you focus on two things: starting and stopping of your air flow using your diaphragm muscle and learning to hold your gesture through the silence. The decision to pause for effect is mental, but the execution is purely physical.

Clearly curious. You should not concern yourself with covering up the fact that something may not be totally clear to you. This can be a very disarming quality to project in a discussion. It invites further engagement and shows a willingness to learn and grow. However, using the words, "I am unclear . . . " about something in the discussion can seem like a negative judgment of another's delivery. That truly might have been the case. Better opening phrases might be, "I was wondering . . . " or "Have you considered . . . ?" They don't direct judgment and show a healthy respect for the perspective of others. It keeps the lines of communication open and flowing. This approach fosters willingness in others to assist you in developing a deeper understanding. After all, they are part of your team!

Phoning it in. It can be difficult to convince yourself that you need to follow the same discipline when talking business over the phone as when you're talking in person. None of the usual visual aspects of a meeting are in place. There is no body language to observe; there is no eye contact to maintain or facial expressions to enhance the delivery of your message. You need to remain true to good speech technique, especially when you're either speaking one on one or participating in a conference call. Although your gestures, eye contact, and facial expressions are not revealed when talking on the phone, they do have a positive effect on your voice. Forward momentum has to be established immediately both physically and mentally. Always prepare your agenda before starting a call; don't pick up the phone unless you can clearly communicate your perspective out loud before participating in the call. Try slowly moving around the room while on the phone as a way to generate additional physical forward momentum. Breathe deliberately as you would in a one-on-one meeting. Make sure you gesture as if your listeners are present in the room. Don't stare off into space. Direct your eye contact to a specific spot in the room, and return to that spot when reinforcing a point. Smile when necessary, but don't overdo it. Disingenuous smiling can color the sound of your voice and make it sound as if you're placating and not engaging.

Seven-layer cake. To persuade someone is actually to allow them to make a decision. You can't force them to make the decision; that would be coercion. What you can do is use your speech technique to deliver a compelling narrative that your listeners can relate to. You will never reach a level of consistent persuasion unless you go through the following seven steps during each interaction. Executives understand some of these steps intuitively, but most are learned through years of trial and error. When using the following list, remember that the order is important! By the way, you can't skip any of the steps.

1. Breathe for authenticity.
2. Gesture for a level of commitment.
3. Know what you want from the interaction.
4. Clearly state your bumper sticker.
5. Present a strong framework.
6. Watch for the connections by reading body language.
7. Build on the trust with active listening.

1—Don't be afraid to expose your deliberate breathing to your listeners. The body language of deliberate breathing sends a message of thoughtfulness and importance. You will be perceived as truly considering your words! When the level of your perceived commitment is high, you will be taken more seriously.

2—Comfort and ease with gesturing not only increases your perceived level of commitment, it also increases your comfort by grounding you in your body. Coordinating your gestures with your breathing aligns your body with your spoken thoughts in a very powerful way.

3—Dare to dream big. Ask yourself the question, "What do I want from this particular interaction?" Become comfortable with the awareness that, in order to be truly successful, something that you believe in will have to be revealed. Just doing a good job isn't enough. Executives have a vision of the bigger picture and where their perspective fits into it.

4—Politicians have bumper stickers. They use them to help us believe that we know where they stand. Bumper stickers are bold and clear statements that must be spoken out loud. One bumper sticker does not fit all interactions. They can change, but not during an interaction. Executives (and politicians) understand that it is more important to your success to communicate clearly than it is to be flexible. There can be time for flexibility later.

5—Think of presenting a strong framework as building a doorway. The manner in which you deliver your message determines the strength of that doorframe. Commitment is even more important than logic. Your listeners' consideration is their acceptance that the door is solid enough to step into. Make sure you step back to allow individuals to enter. Build it and they will come.

6—Trusting your speech technique will give you the freedom to then recognize and interpret your listeners' body language. There are several levels of permission and acceptance that can be detected by paying close attention to subtle facial expressions, gestures, and eye contact. These are the signs that will tell you how well your listeners relate to what you're saying. Confidence in your speech technique will allow you to observe without anyone knowing they are truly being watched.

7—As a good leader, the manner in which you listen will also always be on display. Having the awareness and the energy to not falter in this regard is crucial in developing your Executive Presence. Your eye contact, facial expressions, posture, and gestures must communicate that you are clearly "in the moment" and engaged. Show the same respect when listening that you expect from others when it's your time to speak.

Executive—Present! A top business speech goal is to discover and project your own unique brand of Executive Presence. Obviously, you will need to do several things all at once and seamlessly. The smoother you are the more persuasive you can be. A rate of speech that is measured, poised, and well supported will give you the relaxation and comfort you need to project executive-level confidence. Persuasion can only come from delivering a compelling argument. This requires an enormous amount of commitment and perspective, and you will need to use all of the tools in your speech technique toolbox. Empowering yourself with the knowledge that you possess these tools is not enough. Consistent execution can only be achieved by working with each of your speech technique tools everyday.

The journey to become a great speaker and a respected executive is never-ending. I should know; I'm still on that journey. As you develop your unique brand of executive presence, remember to remain gracious in your delivery. A successful executive knows when to push his or her agenda but doesn't push all the time. Stay relaxed, stay diligent, stay confident, and stay disciplined. You are always learning from every individual you encounter. Revisit the concepts and exercises in this book to keep your speech technique refreshed and full of present perspective. There will always be room to grow.

Bibliography

Ailes, Roger. *You Are the Message*. New York: Penguin, 1988.

Apps, Judy. *Voice and Speaking Skills for Dummies*. New York: John Wiley & Sons, 2012.

Atkinson, Max. *Lend Me Your Ears: All You Need to Know About Making Speeches & Presentations*. New York: Oxford University Press, 2005.

Becker, Dennis. *Powerful Presentation Skills*. New York: Business One Irwin Mirror Press, 1993.

Berkley, Susan. *Speak to Influence: How to Unlock the Hidden Power of Your Voice*. Englewood Cliffs, NJ: Campbell Hall Press, 1999.

Berkun, Scott. *Confessions of a Public Speaker*. Sebastopol, CA: O'Reilly Media, 2004.

Berry, Cicely. *Your Voice & How to Use It: The Classic Guide to Speaking with Confidence*. London: Virgin Books, 1995.

Boone, Daniel R. *Is Your Voice Telling On You? How to Find and Use Your Natural Voice*. San Diego, CA: Plural Publishing, 2015.

Boone, Daniel R., Stephen C. McFarlane, Shelley L. Von Berg, and Richard I. Zraick. *The Voice and Voice Therapy*, Ninth Edition. Englewood Cliffs, NJ: Prentice-Hall, 1983.

Brown, Oren L. *Discover Your Voice: How to Develop Healthy Voice Habits*. San Diego, CA: Singular, 1996.

Brown, Steve. *How to Talk So People Will Listen*. Ada, MI: Baker Books, 2014.

Buckley, Reid. *Strictly Speaking*. New York: McGraw-Hill, 1999.

Carnegie, Dale. *How to Develop Self-Confidence and Influence People*. New York: Pocket Books, 1991.

Cialdini, Robert B. *Influence: The Psychology of Persuasion.* New York: Harper Collins, 2007.

Clark, Boyd, and Ron Crossland. *The Leader's Voice: How Your Communication Can Inspire Action and Get Results!* New York: Select Books, 2001.

Collins, Jim. *Good to Great.* New York: HarperBusiness, 2001.

Cooper, Morton. *Winning with Your Voice: 5 Minutes a Day to a More Effective Winning Voice.* Hollywood, FL: Frederick Fell Publishers, 1990.

Cooper Ready, Anne. *Off the Cuff: What to Say at a Moment's Notice.* Wayne, NJ: Career Press, 2004.

Copeland, Lewis. *The World's Great Speeches.* Mineola, NY: Dover Publications, 1999.

Covey, Stephen. *7 Habits of Highly Effective People.* New York: Simon & Schuster, 2013.

Decker, Bert. *You've Got to Be Believed to Be Heard: The Complete Book of Speaking . . . in Business and in Life!* New York: St. Martins Press, 1991.

Duarte, Nancy. *Slideology: The Art and Science of Creating Great Presentations.* Sebastopol, CA: O'Reilly Media, 2008.

Erard, Michael. *Um . . .: Slips Stumbles, and Verbal Blunders, and What They Mean.* New York: Random House, 2008.

Esposito, Janet. *In the Spotlight: Overcome Your Fear of Public Speaking and Performing.* Southbury, CT: Strong Books, 2000.

Foss, Sonja K. *Inviting Transformation: Presentational Speaking for a Changing World.* Long Grove, IL: Waveland Press, 1993.

Fujishin, Randy. *The Natural Speaker.* Boston, MA: Pearson Education, 1996.

Glass, Lillian J. *Talk to Win.* New York: Perigee Trade, 1988.

Hoff, Ron. *I Can See You Naked: A Fearless Guide to Making Great Presentations.* Riverside, NJ: Andrews McMeel Publishing, 1992.

Humes, James C. *Speak Like Churchill, Stand Like Lincoln: 21 Powerful Secrets of History's Greatest Speakers.* Rocklin, CA: Prima Publishing, 2002.

Jacobi, Henry N. *Building Your Best Voice.* Upper Saddle River, NJ: Prentice Hall, 1982.

Kaye, Jezra. *Speak Like Yourself . . . No Really! Follow Your Strengths and Skills to Great Public Speaking.* New York: 3 Ring Press, 2012.

Linklater, Kristin. *Freeing the Natural Voice.* New York: Drama Publishers, 1976.

Lloyd-Huges, Sarah. *How to Be Brilliant at Public Speaking: Any Audience, Any Situation.* Carlsbad, CA: Hay House, 2007.

Mandel, Steve. *Effective Presentation Skills.* Menlo Park, CA: Crisp Publications, 1993.

McAfee, Barbara, and Peter Block. *Full Voice: The Art and Practice of Vocal Presence.* San Francisco: Berrett-Koehler, 2011.

McCallion, Michael. *The Voice Book*. London: Faber and Faber Ltd., 1998.

McClosky, David Blair. *Your Voice at Its Best: Enhancement of the Healthy Voice, Help for the Troubled Voice*. Long Grove, IL: Waveland Press, Inc., 2011.

Monarth, Harrison, and Larina Kase. *The Confident Speaker: Beat Your Nerves and Communicate at Your Best in Any Situation*. New York: McGraw Hill, 2007.

Morgan, Nick. *Trust Me: Four Steps to Authenticity and Charisma*. San Francisco: Jossey-Bass, 2008.

Morgan, Scott. *Speaking about Science: A Manual for Creating Clear Presentations*. Cambridge, UK: Cambridge University Press, 2006.

Morrison, Malcolm. *Clear Speech: Practical Speech Correction and Voice Improvement*. London: A&C Black, 1996.

Navarro, Joe. *What Every BODY Is Saying: AN Ex-FBI Agent's Guide to Speed-Reading People*. New York: HarperCollins Publishers, 2008.

Noonan, Peggy. *On Speaking Well: How to Give a Speech with Style, Substance, and Clarity*. New York: Simon & Schuster, 2013.

Norcross, John C. *Changeology*. New York: Simon & Schuster, 2013.

Oliver, Robert T. *History of Public Speaking in America*. Boston: Allyn and Bacon, 1970.

Patterson, Kerry, Joseph Grenny, Ron McMillan, and Al Switzler. *Crucial Conversations: Tools for Talking When Stakes Are High*. New York: McGraw Hill, 2002.

Pease, Barbara, and Allan Pease. *The Definitive Book of Body Language*. New York: Bantam, 2006.

Peikoff, Leonard. *Objective Communication: Writing, Speaking, and Arguing*. New York: NAL, 2013.

Pink, Daniel H. *To Sell Is Human: The Surprising Truth About Moving Others*. New York: Riverhead Books, 2012.

Pittampalli, Al. *Read Before Our Next Meeting*. New York: Penguin, 2011.

Pittampalli, Al. *Persuadable*. New York: HarperBusiness, 2016.

Raybould, Simon. *The Little Big Voice: Voice Coaching for Ordinary People*. Carlisle, UK: Piquant Editions, Ltd., 2002.

Rodenburg, Patsy. *Presence*. New York: Penguin Books, 2009.

Rodgers, Janet. *The Complete Voice and Speech Workout*. Milwaukee, WI: Applause Theatre and 8 Cinema Books, 2002.

Romm, Joseph J. *Language Intelligence: Lessons on Persuasion from Jesus, Shakespeare, Lincoln, and Lady Gaga*. Createspace Independent Publishing Platform, London: Franklin Watts, 2005.

Smith, Paul. *Lead with a Story: A Guide to Crafting Business Narratives That Captivate, Convince, and Inspire*. New York: Amacom, 2012.

SpeechWorks. *The Greatest Speeches of All-Time*. Ashland, OR: Blackstone Audio Inc., 2016.

Stuttard, Marie. *The Power of Speech: Effective Techniques for Dynamic Communication*. New York: Barron's Educational Series, 1997.

Walters, Lilly. *Secrets of Successful Speakers*. New York: McGraw Hill, 1993.

Weissman, Jerry. *Presenting to Win: The Art of Telling Your Story*. Upper Saddle River, NJ: Prentice-Hall, 2006.

Wilson, Joni. *The 3-Dimensional Business Voice: The Voice of Command*. Alaska, USA: Blue Loon Press, 2001.

Wilson, Joni. *The 3-Dimensional Voice: A Fun & Easy Method of Voice*. San Diego, CA: Blue Loon Press, 2000.

Index

About the Author

Paul Geiger is a senior associate instructor at New York Speech Coaching in New York City. He specializes in effective business communications. Geiger uses his training, his experience, and, more importantly, his intuition to figure out the key action steps that work for each individual client. He has spent most of his life developing consistent approaches that work for many difficult business communications scenarios. He has enjoyed a parallel career as a voice artist and performer. His radio and television voiceover clients include Mazda, Capital One, and America On Line. Geiger's live and on-camera performances have promoted such companies as Platinum Technologies, Coldwell Banker, and Bacardi International. He is a regular contributor to the website Vocal Articles. *Better Business Speech: Techniques, Tricks, and Shortcuts for Public Speaking at Work* is his first book.